CONSIDER the SQUIRREL

A Collection of Modern-day Parables

REVISED VERSION

Bobby Coleman

ISBNs: 979-8-9927288-0-4 (paperback)

979-8-9927288-1-1 (ebook)

Contents

Foreword

Several years ago I was teaching my congregation on a Sunday morning when, at the beginning of my message, I asked the congregation a question and looked for volunteers to give answers. I had noticed that a particular gentleman was sitting in the front of the church and had been listening with rapt attention. When I asked the responsive question, he immediately shot his hand up with an enthusiasm that was impossible to ignore.

I walked over and held out the interview microphone, interested in hearing what he might share. Immediately, he began sharing an experience he had earlier that week with a squirrel running in front of his car. Honestly, my first thoughts were, "Uh oh. Big mistake to play karaoke on a Sunday with an unknown person. What is he doing talking about hitting a squirrel?"

Those thoughts were quickly dismissed as this man explained how God had used his experience to teach him a personal parable: "consider the squirrel." By the time he concluded his testimony, the entire congregation applauded and verbally expressed praise to God for the wisdom they had heard. I thought to myself, "This guy is gifted to tell spiritual stories!"

Later I was to discover that Bobby Coleman had more than one parable to share. We are fortunate that Bobby obeyed the leading of the Holy Spirit and took the time to write these parables down for the benefit of the body of Christ.

This book is a wonderful tool for inspiring vision, recovering from disappointment, and seeing life from God's point of view. The chapter and section exercises are more than the typical reflections. They are powerful resources that have the potential to help anyone build a road map for personal growth and success in life and ministry.

It is well written and easy to read, though deeply impacting in its content. You could read *Consider the Squirrel* quickly. But I recommend reading it one chapter at a time, with a Bible, pen, and pad of paper in hand. You will get the most out of these modern "parables" by making it a part of your daily meditations and personal devotions. You will be immeasurably enhanced by doing this.

I have come to know Bobby as a devoted husband, father, and believer in Jesus Christ. Now you are going to learn—in the stories he has presented so beautifully in this volume—that God has a lot to say to us through him. Get ready to "cross the road" and experience the abundant life God has designed for you.

Pastor John R. Carter
Lead Pastor of Abundant Life Christian Center, Syracuse, NY
Author of *The Transformed Life*

Preface

My desire to write a book of "modern day parables" has been in the making for almost twenty years, and it really began to take form in me back when I was a children's pastor. Many times throughout the years, I really just gave in to the thought, "I just flat-out missed God," concerning the writing of this book. My desire and drive to get busy and follow God's plan for *Consider the Squirrel* really took place after I received a greater understanding about the difference between "time" and "timing."

The understanding of timing came as I was going over my notes from a teaching series called "The Laws that Govern Your Destiny." That series contained an exercise about discovering one's purpose and governing values in life.

Without that revelation on timing and an incident one Sunday morning late in 2010 when I testified before my congregation about my own discoveries, this book might not have been written, much less published.

While you will find that not everything you read will apply for the particular day or season in which you might find yourself, but everything will apply at the proper time.

"To everything there is a season, and a time for every matter or purpose under Heaven" (Ecclesiastes 3:1 AMP). This was actually the Scripture quotation given at my high school graduation ceremony back in 1981, and it is more relevant to me now than it was then.

I wasn't a Christian then, but God knew I would be. I'm convinced it's the same for you; there are many things that take place in our lives that might not make sense now but will later, with God's timing.

This book is all about discovery—discovering more about *who God is* and, with His help, zeroing in on *who you are*—not what you do, not where you live, not where you work or who you're married to, even if you are or were. I mean *who you are when all that is stripped away*. The real you, the you on the inside!

All that stuff could be totally messed up right now or all perfectly pulled together. Neither situation represents who you really are; all of that has more to do with your skills and abilities and the other externals of life, but they do not define *who you are*. That has to come from the Holy Spirit as God reveals, and if you're not sure what I mean by that, it's one of the things you will discover as you read the book.

The short stories, testimonies, and teachings contained in this book have been prayerfully written to help you define and discover who you really are. To cause you to become more God-conscious and then more self-conscious from His point of view, so that you can realize your fullest potential, live your life with purpose, and find the strength to shake off all the hindrances that hold you back.

You will also find a faith declaration at the end of each chapter. It's a corresponding action to what you've just read. I wrote them with the intent that you would speak them out loud, to declare what you will do with what you just read. Its purpose is to point you in a direction that moves you forward, because without a deliberate pursuit of your purpose and the discovery of God's plan for your life, quite possibly nothing in your life will really change. I pray that this book will provide you with the insight God has for you.

Introduction

Parable? I know we usually don't use words that we associate with the Bible in our everyday conversations, and many of you might not even know what a parable is. A parable—like its better-known cousin, the fable—is a short story with a moral, but a fable is further defined as untrue and more commonly associated with fairy tales, which is why you can find fables of knights fighting dragons, geese laying golden eggs, and so on.

A parable, on the other hand, is derived from the Greek root *para*, which means side by side or next to[1]; the Greek word *parabole* means to compare.[2] Another interesting thing about parables is that they generally have a dual literary expression of realism and symbolism.

This is the reason why Jesus taught with parables. He used everyday examples of sowing and reaping, things lost and found, finances, marriages, banquets, and people such as shepherds, land owners, and employers and laborers because they were immediately relatable to people.

On one particular occasion as Jesus began to teach, He asked those gathered around Him "How can I describe the kingdom of God? What story should I use to illustrate it?" (Mark 4:30 NLT). Jesus used real symbolism of their everyday lives to expand and correct their understanding about God with the things they could most relate to. He challenged them to see beyond what they had learned by tradition and by the teachings of the religious leaders of the day, who had brought much

---

1. Thayer and Smith, "Greek Lexicon entry for *Para*," The NAS New Testament Greek Lexicon, 1999. http://www.biblestudytools.com/lexicons/greek/nas/para.html (accessed June 24, 2014).
2. Thayer and Smith, "Greek Lexicon entry for *Parabole*," The NAS New Testament Greek Lexicon, 1999. http://www.biblestudytools.com/lexicons/greek/nas/parabole.html (accessed June 24, 2014).

confusion and even fear into the worship of God through burdensome rules and rituals.

Jesus reintroduced God to them as a loving and just Father, and I believe we need to do the same again today. I come across people constantly who are just as confused about who God is now as those Jesus ministered to nearly 2,000 years ago.

Second Corinthians says, "Satan, who is the god of this world, has blinded the minds of those who don't believe" (2 Corinthians 4:4 NLT). Satan, along with the religious and secular culture of today, has made the spiritual landscape more confusing than ever. Religious leaders have introduced many versions and ideas about who God is and what He wants and expects from us. Jesus made it plain and singular. Jesus told them, "I am the way, the truth, and the life. No one can come to the Father except through me" (John 14:6 NLT).

I've written this book using the same parabolic methods Jesus used, because I know life's real occurrences can and do reveal the heart of God and the workings of His kingdom. So let's see where we can expand and correct our understanding of God in much the same way today as Jesus' listeners did then.

For those of you who discover the love of God for the first time while reading this book, you can turn to chapter 20 at any time and find a prayer to guide you in your acceptance of salvation and faith in Jesus.

So let's get going: *The kingdom of God is like…*

Section I: Moving Forward

Chapter 1: Consider the Squirrel

There is a way that seems right to a man, but its end is the
way of death.
—Proverbs 16:25

One day as I was driving to work, taking a shortcut down a back country road, a squirrel ran out in front of me. He was still quite a ways ahead, but I could see him clearly. He ran out past the yellow line and about halfway across the opposite lane and stopped. He sat up on his hind legs and looked at me coming toward him with his tail snapping up and down.

I know you can picture this; it happens all the time. As I got closer, he got back down on all four legs, looked back and forth, and just as I got there, he headed right back where he came from. Yep, you guessed it—I clipped him. As I looked in the rearview mirror, I could see him lying there; his tail was still twitching.

My first response was anger: "You stupid squirrel! What did you do that for?"

Then God spoke to me: "Consider the squirrel." Those three words were all I heard, but I knew instantly what God meant.

Many times as we set out to attempt something new, we act a lot like that squirrel. We start out boldly and quickly. After all, we're excited. But then as we see opposition or our plan seems to be taking longer than we wanted, we start to question ourselves; and rather than continue that last little bit to get across the road, we panic, second-guess ourselves, and turn back to the familiar. Thankfully, we don't suffer the same fate as my squirrel friend did, but we do die a little bit with each failed attempt.

Consider the Squirrel

I'd like to challenge you right now to do the following exercise; it's exactly how I "considered the squirrel," and I believe it could bring great satisfaction to your life as you do it now too.

Consider the Squirrel Exercise, Part I

1. Take out a piece of paper and write down in no particular order all the things you wanted to do, but quit before finishing. I'm not talking about a bucket list of wishes but real-life issues such as quitting a habit, going to college, getting in shape, etc. Don't think about it too hard; just write.

2. Now add to your list those things you have wanted to do, but have put no effort into. Again, don't over-think or spiritualize this; just write. (Don't be concerned if you find yourself getting emotional about this. Just keep going.)

3. When you are satisfied with your list, go back through and number the items from highest to lowest priority. This might change several times, but work at it until you believe they are in the right order.

4. Set your new list aside for the moment and read on; we will come back to it at the end of this chapter.

Making a list of things that we've wanted to do but haven't yet can be discouraging, so for the moment set aside any negative emotions and just imagine seeing the items on your list through to completion. Relish in the satisfaction that you did it. Now capture those thoughts. This is your vision!

The book of Habakkuk, like many other Old Testament books, was named after the prophet who wrote it. His name means "he who embraces or holds on to." It implies grabbing hold of something or someone, even in the middle of a struggle, and refusing to let go.

Although he first struggled with what he saw around him and God's response to it, Habakkuk eventually came to trust God completely. He called out to the Lord and asked God two questions, and then declared:

I will stand my watch and set myself on the rampart, and watch to see what He will say to me, and what I will answer when I am corrected. Then the Lord answered me and said: "Write the vision and make it plain on tablets, that he may run who reads it. For the vision is yet for an appointed time; but at the end it will speak, and it will not lie. Though it tarries, wait for it; because it will surely come, it will not tarry (Habakkuk 2:1-3 NKJV).

When God answered Habakkuk, He gave him specific instructions: *Write down what I tell you and make it plain for all to see and understand, so that they who read it can grasp hold of it and do it.* Remember, Habakkuk's name means "to embrace or holds on to," and that is what I want to challenge you to do now. Grab hold of your future just like I had to do, and then wrestle or fight to see it come to pass.

Before I could write this book, I had to create the vision for it and embrace it as truly possible. I had to see myself typing out these pages, but if I had stopped there, I would have only embraced a dream. A vision, on the other hand, requires corresponding actions, so I did what I am about to share with you; I had to embrace the moment, take action, and when necessary I had to speak to myself and declare, "I will finish what I've started." The overall vision for this book was my *embracing moment,* and you are reading my corresponding actions!

So how do we get to *your embracing moment* and your corresponding actions? Look at your list of unfinished or yet-to-start goals. If you're still fiddling with the prioritizing, that's okay. We're going to tackle them one at a time.

Consider the Squirrel Exercise, Part II

1. Look at the first item on your list, and again in your mind's eye, see it through to completion and sense the joy of accomplishment. Embrace this vision.

2. Now in no particular order, quickly write down those things that it will take to make this come to pass—no excuses, no limitations,

just write. Your list might include what you will stop doing in order to reach that thing as well. For example, getting out of debt will mean doing some new things and stopping some old things such as overspending or impulse buying; quitting smoking may mean creating new routines, etc. These are your corresponding actions.

3. Now take your vision and your corresponding actions and embrace them as fully possible. Don't consider whatever it was that caused you to turn back to the familiar before. Rather, look forward toward God, for He is the God of the second chance (and third and fourth and fiftieth).

Now with your vision in front of you, don't just try it again. Do it this time. Expect a battle, wrestle with your circumstances, fight your emotions and fears, grab hold of your vision, and refuse to let go of it. Be tenacious and accept no excuses, especially from yourself. In spite of all that you may be facing, regardless of your finances, situations, or present circumstances, there are things you can begin to do even now.

For example, if you have no money to invest in your goal, develop the discipline you will need when you have the finances that will surely come. How, you ask? Start with what you already have; exercise discipline in what you have before you now. Keep your room or house clean, get to work on time, take care of the possessions you have now, and be faithful.

Developing discipline is free and pays huge dividends later! "I can do all things through Christ who strengthens me" (Philippians 4:13). Don't trivialize even the smallest effort; just build on it and make it grow until you realize all that you have embraced and grabbed hold of. Speak out of your own mouth, *I can do all things through Christ who strengthens me,* every time you think of turning around and running back across the road.

Remember what God said to Habakkuk: "…If it seems slow in coming, wait patiently, for it will surely take place. It will not be delayed" (Habakkuk 2:3 NLT). Don't quit; keep moving forward even when it seems that nothing is changing. Wait for it; it will surely come!

Commit your vision to God in prayer. It's as simple as, "Lord, I need Your help to do this." Count on His strength to see you through and then get started. I did, and the book in your hands is proof that you can do it, too.

So consider the squirrel. Don't turn back to the familiar. Don't quit on your corresponding actions. Get across to the other side!

Faith Declaration: I believe I can do all things through Christ who strengthens me, so I choose to move forward. I am not a quitter, I am not easily discouraged, I am not afraid of the new, and I declare I will not return to the familiar. I forsake those things that have kept me bound from fulfilling my purpose and destiny in God.

Chapter 2: Direction, Not Perfection

The steps of a good man are ordered by the Lord, and He delights in his way. Though he fall, he shall not be utterly cast down; for the Lord upholds him with His hand.
—Psalm 37:23-24

The kingdom of God is like a man who, upon seeing fresh footprints in the snow, set out to step perfectly into each print in front of him. At first, following along in each footstep seemed rather easy. But after a time, here and again, he just slightly missed the mark and made a misstep. Others came along and they, too, had similar success and failure until at last the footprints were no more; instead, there was just a clearly marked, packed-down, narrow path.

Some of you already get the meaning of this. But for the rest of us, let's go over it as I first explained it to a friend. We were talking on the phone, and he said he was quite frustrated about an issue he was dealing with and what he thought was a lack of measurable progress. He was very upset and telling me he felt like if he didn't do everything perfectly and hold it all together, then he would ultimately fail.

As he was telling me of his struggle, I happened to be looking out the window because it was snowing very hard. I was really at a loss for words; but as I looked out across the fresh snow, God put an image in my mind, and immediately I knew what to say. God isn't looking for perfection from us, He's looking for direction. I knew I had to explain myself, for my friend had no idea what God had just showed me.

So I asked him, "Do you remember when we were kids and we'd go outside after a fresh snowstorm and everything seemed so clean and bright? Remember the times we'd see a solitary set of footprints in the snow and follow them to see where they were going? Remember how

19

we'd try to step exactly into each print but eventually lose our balance or something and miss? Then, as each of us followed along, eventually enough of us missed the steps in front of us until we had just packed down a narrow little path through the snow?" Before he could answer, I added, "But we all got to wherever the original set of tracks led to, right?"

I was sure by his hesitation that he still wasn't sure where I was going with this, so I continued, "That's how it is with God. There's only been one perfect man on the earth, and that was Jesus. He makes the footprints in the snow, and we follow them all the way home. Jesus said, 'I am the way, the truth, and the life. No one comes to the Father except through Me'" (John 14:6).

Our goal in life isn't to be *perfect* but *perfected,* and that's more about living our lives with consistency in our direction and excellence in our attitude concerning the things of God rather than doing any one thing perfectly. The apostle Paul addressed this very issue and its effect on his own life.

> Not that I have already attained, or am already *perfected*; but I press on, that I may lay hold of that for which Christ Jesus has also laid hold of me. Brethren, I do not count myself to have apprehended; but one thing I do, forgetting those things which are behind and reaching forward to those things which are ahead, I press toward the goal for the prize of the upward call of God in Christ Jesus (Philippians 3:12-14).

Paul understood that we are in a process of being perfected, and that we will not always do everything correctly. This is why he continued by stating he didn't count himself as already having it all together yet. But rather than getting frustrated and quitting, he chose to forget those things that were behind him and press on toward the goal—the upward call of God in Christ Jesus.

When we set our hearts to follow Jesus as Paul did, the reality is that we, too, will fail at times and come up short; our desire to press forward in life will not come without opposition, and there will even be times when our own poor choices sabotage our future. The key is not to panic, but to regain our focus and direction and keep stepping into the tracks ahead of us.

God isn't looking for absolute perfection in what we do; He knows that's unattainable for us. He wants us to be willing to follow His leading based on our relationship with Him and walk with consistency in our lives. Just like the footprints in the snow, we may end up with a narrow path from so many missteps, but we won't lose our way to the end; we will get there just like they did in the parable we read. This can only come by a dogged determination to stay consistent in our direction as laid out by the Lord; it does not mean doing everything completely perfect or without failure, because failure is an unfortunate byproduct of being born into a fallen world.

Whenever I get discouraged by my own failures, I have to check my attitude before it runs away with me and choose not to be influenced by how I feel or by what I can see around me. I must remember that God is looking for consistency in my growth and direction—not absolute perfection.

Henry Ford said, "Failure is just an opportunity to begin again more intelligently." So then, failure is only final if we quit, and we dealt with that in Chapter One. Success doesn't come through the absence of failure; it comes to us by the absence of quitting! Now that you have embraced a vision and have committed to a new way of doing things, don't fear failing at times or making the occasional misstep. Just determine in your heart to focus on a forward direction with God which doesn't included quitting.

Abraham Lincoln is credited with doing amazing things for America and is regarded as one of our greatest presidents, but often lost in all his accolades is the account of the tremendous amount of failure he overcame to become who we recognize him to be. Winston Churchill was another great statesman who endured long bouts of failures and extreme testing in his lifetime; he is credited with the following quote: "Success is going from failure to failure without loss of enthusiasm." This reveals and demonstrates the prevailing attitude he held in life. We must hold a similar one to enjoy our own successes.

Consider the Squirrel

There is a big difference between "a spirit of excellence" and "a spirit of perfection." A spirit of excellence is doing everything you do with an attitude of putting forth your best effort, regardless of circumstances and with great attention to detail. A spirit of perfection, however, is based on a judgmental and critical attitude that nothing's ever really good enough, which usually breeds frustration and a failure mentality.

Both approaches affect the way we think (our attitude), which in turn affects how we act (our habits). Habits are formed by repeated actions, so it stands to reason that a critical spirit of perfection is ultimately the habit of failure. Our determination must be to habitually operate in and be motivated by a spirit of excellence so we can head in the consistent direction that God has laid out for us.

You've got to learn to operate in this way of thinking, especially in tough times, just as the apostle Paul did when he said, "But one thing *I do,* forgetting those things which are behind and reaching forward to those things which are ahead, I press toward the goal…" (Philippians 3:13-14). Don't allow yourself to get trapped in the "I have to hold it all together" mentality. God is the one who holds it all together, whether we can understand it all or not. Your part is to hold on to the vision and goals you have now determined to pursue in your life based on God's leading, and continue to support them with *your corresponding actions.*

Our ultimate goal in life has to be to participate in God's redemptive plan. First John pretty much makes this plain for us: "But whoever keeps His word, truly the love of God is *perfected* in him. By this we know that we are in Him. He who says he abides in Him ought himself also to *walk just as He walked*" (1 John 2:5-6).

We walk in Jesus' footprints when we determine to keep God's Word and allow Him to perfect us even in the middle of life's struggles. So follow the footsteps of the Lord, and when you make a misstep remember that being perfected is a part of God's redemptive plan for us. It's all about direction.

Faith Declaration: Today I put my focus on direction. I am determined to know the will of God for my life and to follow in the Master's footsteps. I believe that Jesus is the way, the truth, and the life, and therefore I confess that I will follow Jesus in the way, I will seek to know the truth, and I will live the life God has intended for me to live, free from condemnation and free of the fear of failure!

Chapter 3: Imagine That!

But as it is written: "Eye has not seen, nor ear heard, Nor have entered into the heart of man The things which God has prepared for those who love Him." But God has revealed them to us through His Spirit. For the Spirit searches all things, yes, the deep things of God. For what man knows the things of a man except the spirit of the man which is in him? Even so no one knows the things of God except the Spirit of God. Now we have received, not the spirit of the world, but the Spirit who is from God, that we might know the things that have been freely given to us by God.
—1 Corinthians 2:9-12

As a former children's pastor, I can tell you that one of the greatest challenges to conducting a successful service was keeping our children's and teenager's attention. Our services were pretty cutting-edge at the time, because we used multiple stimulation techniques in unison to keep the kids on the edge of their seat and engaged. In our children's sanctuary, we built bleachers and stadium-style seating so the kids seemed like they were right on top of each other and crammed in. We did this to create anticipation.

Against the back of the stage, we built a wall with multiple openings at various levels for the surprise popping-in of any number of characters at orchestrated times. In the middle of a point that I was making, we would have puppets or people or characters in full costume seem to interrupt what I was doing. They would walk across the stage carrying on a conversation or open the shutters on a window and start singing or talking. This went on for more than an hour every Sunday, and at the end of it we were all exhausted.

25

Consider the Squirrel

It was deliberately orchestrated chaos, and our purpose behind it all was to reinforce our central Bible theme of the day. We worked our theme into each segment, skit, and every other seemingly-distracting episode throughout the service. We knew we had to be fast-paced, ever-changing, and exciting to keep their attention and capture their imaginations.

A child's attention span is roughly one minute per year of age up until about the age of twelve or thirteen, which is when it somewhat plateaus. I used to study quite a bit about how to keep a child's attention and found that when you watch a children's television program, for example, you will see that approximately every three minutes or less the segments or characters change what they are doing. This is because every segment change clears the attention meter in a child's brain, and as each new segment begins, so does the ticking on the attention-meter clock. In order to create continuous segment changes, we also used videos, games, role-playing segments, and illustrated object lessons to drive home the central theme of the day.

Another important aspect of our services focused on the power of imagination. Even now as adults, we learn and think the way we did as children, especially when it comes to how we create thought. By that I mean we create thoughts by pictures in our minds, and what we can imagine, we don't think in words.

For example, you don't see a "pink elephant" even when you read the words. Your imagination kicks in, and then you see a pink elephant. I want you to grab a friend or family member and have them do the following exercise. You will read and lead them through it. I call it, "Imagine that!"

Imagine That Exercise

1. Have your friend or family member stand up with their feet shoulder-width apart and lift their arm straight out in front of them. Tell them to point at an object directly across the room. This is their starting point.

2. Keeping their arm straight out and their finger pointing at their starting point, have them keep their feet planted and their arm straight out and rotate their torso, swinging their arm and pointer finger backward until they choose to stop. Have them point at an object behind them; have them focus on the object for a moment. This is their stopping point. Now have them rotate back around.

3. Still looking straight ahead, have them put their arm down to their side and do the following portion of this exercise with their eyes closed and without moving.

4. In their mind's eye, have them just visualize that they are doing this next part, but don't have them actually do it.

5. Tell them in their mind's eye to lift their arm up as they did in the beginning and point at their starting point. Remind them to keep their eyes closed; they should be standing still and only picturing this in the imagination.

6. Now in their mind's eye, tell them to rotate backward and see the object of their stopping point. Once they've done this, tell them to see themselves rotating two feet farther beyond their stopping point.

7. Now, still with their eyes closed, have them imagine they turned back around like they did in the beginning, and have them imagine doing steps 4 through 6 a second time with this change. This time when they rotate backward have them see their stopping point and then imagine rotating four or more feet past their stopping point.

8. Okay, last step. Once again, with their eyes open, do the exercise again from the beginning—have them lift their arm, point straight ahead, and rotate to their stopping point and then to their new end point four or more feet beyond that.

If they were able to do this correctly, then they probably were able to rotate and go beyond their original stopping point another four or more feet—much farther than they first did on their own. Imagining going the extra distance first and then actually doing it is the power of your imagination. It's talking to your brain in the language it understands. Pictures and imaginations are brainspeak!

One of the many ways God would use my teaching gift in the children's ministry was to give me the ability to break down words so that children could recognize and understand them more fully. In this case, the word "imagination" could be broken down as "image action" or the doing the things you see.

You, by your imagination and ability to create a vision of doing something in your mind's eye, told your brain that you could do it, and so you did. My coaching helped you paint a picture in your mind that your imagination illustrated as an image action, and then your brain grasped the concept as a real possibility and did it.

Of course, no amount of picturing yourself flying is ever going to lift your feet off the floor, but in the realm of the possible the power of our imagination takes what you first dismiss as impossible and makes it a possibility. Is it possible to be healed even after a dire diagnosis? Is it possible to save a struggling marriage? Is it possible to regain your footing after a financial collapse? Anything like this is possible.

Sure, you can do this without God. The exercise you just did was only to show you the power of your imagination. God created your brain and the way it functions, so when you apply this principle to your faith, you are really on to something. "The things which are impossible with men are possible with God," (Luke 18:27). God just might have known about this before we did, and looking at Scripture with this in mind sure can make you look at things with a much greater degree of possibility.

"Now faith is the substance of things hoped for, the evidence of things not seen," (Hebrews 11:1). So where does faith begin? In the realm of God's possibilities, not humanity's! When it comes to receiving by faith, God is the coach who walks us through this exercise and causes us to reach beyond what we could do on our own. Faith becomes the substance, the evidence, of things not seen except in our mind's eye. First God paints the picture, and then when we are convinced because we can see it, we grasp hold of it and do it.

Whenever we start something new, we definitely will come to our stopping point, but this point might be quite a ways short of our actual abilities and our ending point, as illustrated by the exercise we just did. This is where our faith becomes the evidence of things not seen. When we allow God to teach us and paint a picture in our imagination for us, we can go farther than we first thought possible.

I've heard people encourage others by saying, "See yourself healed," "See yourself prosperous," or in my case, "See yourself writing that book." This is the starting point. Faith takes corresponding actions, according to the Bible, and steps out to go beyond our personally-set stopping points. It has taken plenty of faith for me to reach my ending point, which was handing this book over to my editor.

What do you dream about? What consumes your thoughts? What do you want to do or become? Don't make excuses, but make the impossible the very possible through God and by faith. Have a vision, an image action for your future and destiny; point at it and then go for it. When you come to your stopping point, remember you are not at your end!

Talk your brain's language, dream big, don't limit God, and expect setbacks and failures along the way. Thomas Edison failed nearly a thousand times before he got the light bulb right. If it makes you feel good or encourages you any, he also blew up or burned down his lab several times during the process. He only saw these things as stopping points; the end result was the light bulb!

One last thing about Edison: He was asked once about how he invented so many things and held so many patents. His answer was perfectly fitting for our discussion here. He said, "Through all the years of experimenting and research, I never once made a discovery. I started where the last man left off."[3] Edison took other folks' concepts—their visions and imaginations, if you will—to the ending point because they stopped!

It's not some cheesy mind-over-matter psycho baloney I'm encouraging you to do; I'm asking you to take the very powerful gift

3. Wikiquote contributors, "Thomas Edison," Wikiquote, , http://en.wikiquote.org/w/index. php?title=Thomas_Edison&oldid=1746843 (accessed June 24, 2014).

of imagination that God has given each of us and use it to its fullest potential.

> Now to Him who is able to do exceedingly abundantly above all that we ask or think, according to the power that works in us, (Ephesians 3:20 NKJV).

Faith Declaration: I will not stop before I reach the end of everything my faith has inspired me to do or become. Then I will go even farther with God's power working in me, because God can do much, much more than anything I can ask or imagine!

Chapter 4: Am I the Seed?

*For as the rain comes down, and the snow from heaven, and
do not return there, but water the earth, and make it bring
forth and bud, that it may give seed to the sower and bread to
the eater, so shall My word be that goes forth from My mouth;
it shall not return to Me void, but it shall accomplish what I
please, and it shall prosper in the thing for which I sent it.*
—Isaiah 55:10-11

One of the purposes of this book, as I stated back in the preface, was for you to discover who you really are, the you who is defined by God's design for your life, so you can live to your full potential and become much more with His help than you could become on your own.

Throughout the next few pages I will use the phrases "process and preparation" and "time and timing" interchangeably because the events that take place in the seasons of our lives are much easier to understand if we label or define them and assign them a purpose.

For years, I couldn't grasp the principles of process and preparation. Whenever I thought I had heard from the Lord in prayer about a certain thing or direction, I just assumed it was for that time and immediately headed out to do it. Big mistake! It took the revelation I spoke about back in the introduction concerning *time* and *timing* for me to finally begin— and I emphasize *begin*—to see what I'm about to share with you.

We all believe we're ready to do great things in life, or be the starter instead of the benchwarmer, long before we really are. But the truth is that with any endeavor, there has to be a time of preparation. When my son, Aaron, made his high school hockey team as a freshman, he was sure he was ready to start over the juniors and seniors on the team. But

31

he wasn't nearly as fast or game savvy as he later became by practicing with the older players every week.

Take, for example, a common cookbook. Most assuredly, one of the things the recipe will contain is how long it will take to *prepare*. The Olympic Games happen on an alternating schedule for the summer and winter games every four years and last a very short two weeks, and yet years—if not lifetimes—of training go into preparing for one event.

Joseph was one of Abraham's twelve sons, and what a process— tossed into a pit by his own jealous brothers, sold as a slave to Potiphar, a captain of the Egyptian guard, then eventually thrown into prison for a crime he didn't commit. All of this was his "prep time" before becoming the prime minster of Egypt. Moses spent nearly forty years in the desert in preparation to deliver Israel from 430 years of bondage.

Paul, already a teacher of the law, spent nearly fifteen years after his conversion being prepared to become the apostle who would write two thirds of the New Testament. Jesus Himself waited nearly thirty years for the perfect timing to begin three years of ministry. What did He do during that time? Luke records, "And Jesus increased in wisdom and stature, and in favor with God and men" (Luke 2:52). The Son of God had a time of preparation, and so will we—regardless of the endeavor.

When I received the thought, nearly twenty years ago, to write this book, it came as a small, almost insignificant passing thought. In actuality it was a seed. The time in between then and now was the process and preparation time, and this book is the harvest or fruit from that seed, which has now matured.

The parable I'm about to share with you I've written from the seed's perspective, and it is in a style I learned and taught from often as a children's pastor. One year for Resurrection Sunday, I dressed up in full Roman centurion garb and told the story of Jesus' crucifixion from the centurion's point of view all the way to his words at the foot of the cross: "So when the centurion and those with him, who were guarding Jesus, saw the earthquake and the things that had happened, they feared greatly, saying, 'Truly this was the son of God!'" (Matthew 27:54 NJKV).

Bobby Coleman

The impact was incredible and very relevant; I pray this parable will have a similar effect on you now and will help to expand your understanding about the need to recognize both time and timing. Remember, "to everything there is a season" (Ecclesiastes 3:1).

I couldn't wait for the day of the harvest. As the summer days passed by, we grew plump and rich with nutrients, each kernel growing to its full potential. On the day of the harvest, we were so excited our day had finally come. Yet as we were pulled from the stalk, we were thrown aside into a dry, dark container. How could this be? We were among the best.

In complete silence and inactivity, I sat until all hope of being used was gone; my ability to nourish was vanishing. I dried up and became hard. And still I sat through the cold of a winter season, seemingly forgotten and discarded.

Then, as a new season began, there was a stirring, and light broke in among us. I thought, "What use could I be now?" Yet I was taken and broken apart. Gently I dropped through the hands of the Master planter into the soil from which I had come. I knew this place; I had been here before. This was the place where I had grown to have such expectations of becoming fruit for the harvest.

As I was covered in the soil, my thoughts conflicted between, "Now I am truly forgotten and dead," and, "This is the place of my beginning." Struggling between my thoughts of abandonment and "This must mean something good because the Master Himself has put me here," I lay covered. My will to live and press on pulled against my thoughts of death; I literally felt as if I were being pulled apart.

The moisture within the soil began to loosen my hardness. Even in this apparent place of death and darkness, my thoughts fluctuated between what I could see and feel all around me and what I sensed within me. Something had to happen, but what?

33

Then, without my complete understanding and when it seemed all hope was gone, water from above washed the soil from me, and light burst forth. I stood up!

Yes, I recognized this place. But this time, I had understanding, purpose, and conviction. I was alive; I had taken in the water and light and had begun to grow again. My purpose was intact; it was my understanding that was lacking!

With growth comes understanding. I was no longer looking to become only the fruit of harvest for one good meal. Yes, with growth comes understanding!

The Master who first chose me at the harvest—it was He who had separated me and set me aside for His purposes. When the time was right, He replanted me in His own fertile soil and nourished me with the water and light of His Word, causing me, through the struggle with my own thoughts of abandonment, to break forth and to grow again into another harvest.

Sometimes we are so certain we know what is best that we become very singular in our focus and rule out the possibility that anything else could be taking place in our lives except what we can understand.

In our parable, the seed had the limited understanding that its sole purpose was to grow up and be used for one good meal. However God's purpose for the seed was to be multiplied so that in each cycle of seed time and harvest the seed could become both seed for a new harvest and nourishment for the current one.

God knows what is best for us, and coming to a place of trust in His ways—much less learning to discern the difference between His time and timing of a thing—isn't always easy, but it is necessary. He alone knows how to use this time of preparation to make us become both "seed for the sower and bread for the eater" to create in us the process that continues to renew us.

Each time we go through this process, much like the seed in our parable we too must come to this conclusion: My vision is too small; God is enlarging me yet again. This process in our lives is about so much more than what we first perceive it to be, and no matter how many times we go through this process there will still be times when we won't catch on very quickly.

Before I began to have a better understanding of process and preparation, there were many times when I was certain that it was a waste of valuable time to just sit and learn or to allow myself to be mentored, or to just be faithful doing what I was doing right where I was. I had no idea this was part of my process and preparation for greater things yet to come in my life, so I despised the small things I was doing as boring, unfulfilling, or beneath my talent level and abilities. My attitude was sabotaging my own growth and ability to be multiplied.

Once I learned to see things from the Lord's perspective, I began to embrace the wisdom of preparation, for it's the place of purified motives, it's the place of forged commitments, and it's the place of self-discovery. It's the place where God anoints us so we can give out and still not be emptied. It's the place of perpetual renewal. And without this process, you eventually will give out and die.

Nothing is worse than getting into the middle of something only to find yourself questioning, "Why am I doing this?" Or worse yet, to allow yourself to become frustrated because you are not receiving the accolades that you think you deserve. These are the things that preparation peels off and exposes, and this must be done before any real progress is made.

It's also the place where we learn that what we are doing today is never just about today; it's where we learn how to appropriate the promises of God for our lives, which usually come in baby steps. What you learn in prayer today is what God builds upon tomorrow. The victories you experience today are to encourage you tomorrow when hope seems lost and victory gone. Just determine not to quit; keep moving forward!

It's where we learn to cry out as David did while speaking to King Saul just before he faced Goliath. "Your servant has killed both lion and bear; and this uncircumcised Philistine will be like one of them, seeing he has defied the armies of the living God…the Lord, who delivered me from the paw of the lion and from the paw of the bear, He will deliver me from the hand of this Philistine" (1 Samuel 17:36-37).

Consider the Squirrel

That kind of confidence comes only through preparation. I won't lie to you—it's not always fun, nor is it easy, and sometimes in the middle of it, if you do not stay diligent and focused, you could become frustrated and give up. Remember this truth: God is always working on our behalf even when we can't see it or sense it.

My certainty of this comes straight from Scripture; James exhorts us: "My brethren, count it all joy when you fall into various trials, knowing that the testing of your faith produces patience. But let patience have its perfect work, that you may be perfect and complete, lacking nothing" (James 1:2-4). When I think of something that is perfect, I think of something being both mature and stable. We all want that in our lives; we just don't really like the process it may take to become that.

So if you find yourself in a place of questioning or impatience—and trust me, any honest person will admit they've been there—it's time to get quiet, stop pushing, and ask God how to cooperate more fully with the Holy Spirit.

God is not holding us back or withholding anything from us, but He is preparing us for life, and life more abundantly.

Faith Declaration: My purpose before God is intact even when my understanding is lacking! I will embrace my times of preparation, for I am confident God is equipping me for every good work according to His purposes and plans for my life. Just as the planted seed eventually becomes the fruit of harvest, my life has a purpose—one that I fully expect God to reveal to me.

Chapter 5: The Grill with the Broken Wheel

If you need wisdom, ask our generous God, and he will give it to you. He will not rebuke you for asking. But when you ask him, be sure that your faith is in God alone. Do not waver, for a person with divided loyalty is as unsettled as a wave of the sea that is blown and tossed by the wind. Such people should not expect to receive anything from the Lord. Their loyalty is divided between God and the world, and they are unstable in everything they do.
—James 1:5-8 NLT

A certain man planned a great feast, which his wife had invited many to attend. On the day of the great barbecue, an unplanned yet welcomed guest arrived. In order to make room for them to sit and enjoy the feast, additional tables had to be set up on the deck, and the grill moved to the front driveway.

As the man began to pull the grill around the house toward the driveway, a wheel fell off, so the man had to stop and put the wheel back on; he was surprised, but put little thought to it and continued. He pushed the grill further, and again the wheel came off, and again he paused to put the wheel on a second time. He now decided to slow down his pace, but as he carefully continued to pull the grill around the garage and toward the driveway, the wheel fell off yet again.

By now the man had become irritated; thinking bad words and beginning to mumble and complain under his breath, he even resented his guests and called his own barbecue "stupid." Though he planned the party and had looked forward to this day, he was now in no mood to celebrate and was angry because of the grill.

The man in this story, as you may have realized, is me. I share this incident with you in the true form of a biblical parable for much the same reason why I believe Jesus Himself used this storytelling method. The quirky, rhythmic flow of parables emphasizes certain points without them necessarily having to be pointed out. In this case, for the sake of our discussion, I want to make clear what that point is. It is the continuous starting, stopping, and starting again that I was compelled to do.

Stay with me now, because we are going somewhere much further than the front yard. Shortly after our big barbecue, my wife Lisa was out of town for the weekend, so I called and asked a friend if he wanted to ride to church together. It's about a 45-minute drive, and as we talked he began telling me about a situation he was dealing with, which quickly turned into him asking me why, when, and how much longer would it be before he would see things change?

As I listened to him talk about his ordeal, I realized he wasn't listening to what he was saying. His actions were not lining up at all with what he said he was doing and trying to achieve. With the grill incident still fresh in my mind, I shared the following observations.

"You know that big grill I have? Well, it's got cheap little plastic wheels, and the other day as I was pulling it through the grass from my backyard to my driveway, one of the wheels fell off *three times*. Each time I had to stop and put the wheel back on, it stopped my forward progress. Each time I tried to adjust the wheel so it would stay on the axle, it caused me to become more and more frustrated."

That day I told my friend what I am telling you today: We are a lot like my grill, and impatience, distractions, selfishness, carelessness, and sometimes just circumstances beyond our control are some of the things that could represent a broken wheel in our own life's journey. Every time one of those things, and others like them, stop us in our tracks, it will take time and work to get us back on course. There are no short cuts to excellence and lasting results in life take time to develop, even when everything is going according to plan. That's certainly the case when, without warning, one of our wheels fall off.

The cares of life demand that we train ourselves to master them, and that can only come from the Lord, which is why Jesus said, "These things have I spoken to you, that in Me you may have peace. In the world you will have tribulation; but be of good cheer, I have overcome the world" (John 16:33).

Here in upstate New York, we have an abundance of apple orchards, and it is amazing to see how an apple tree is pruned; if you didn't know better, you'd think they were cutting the tree back too far and destroying it. But they're not. Apple trees must be kept low to the ground and allowed to spread out so the fruit can be plentiful, as well as easily harvested, each fall.

Sometimes in our own impatience or discomfort with an issue, we can't see or understand the need to have things cut off or pruned back in our lives. We actually revolt against the process because we see it as our destruction rather than as preparation to produce and allow even greater potential to be developed in our lives.

Repentance in this sense is similar to the process of pruning the apple tree in that God uses repentance to have us cut off the very things that hinder us from producing greater growth and abundance in our lives. But repentance is much more than just feeling sorry for something or just getting rid of something—true biblical repentance involves turning away from or cutting away something sinful and turning to God instead.

It's about committing yourself to following after God with consistency in your direction and staying on track. Repentance is God's way of encouraging us to fix our broken wheels so we can continue our journey unhindered.

When we face challenges in our lives, remember the grill with the broken wheel; know that setbacks in life happen, just don't let a setback become a go back!

Don't worry about how long something seems to take or the intensity of the struggle; we will deal with that issue later in the book. For now, determine that the temptations to opt out or take shortcuts are not options and move forward. The final results of process and preparation are worth the time and effort required to bring them to pass in our lives.

Consider the Squirrel

Don't do like I did the day of the barbecue; I became frustrated and angry because of the additional time and effort it was taking to get everything done and forgot the anticipation I had about the party, temporarily ruining my own good time. Don't give up on what God has promised you, even when it seems that the wheels are coming off in your life; rather, have faith and confidence that following through on the wisdom and direction that comes from God will get you where you need to be.

Faith Declaration: I am quick to cooperate with the leadings of the Lord. When I ask for wisdom, He is faithful to give it to me. I allow Him to adjust me and to show me those things that I must let go of to continue my growth. I determine to walk in peace and patience, for I am an overcomer in all things.

Section I Review Page: Moving Forward

The first five chapters of this book were written with a very definite purpose in mind, which I want to review with you now. I have listed them much like a to-do list for the ease of our review. Remember, we are moving forward!

1. To see and recognize the areas where I gave up on myself and my dreams. To make some determinations to move forward and finish those things which I had started, and to boldly see through to completion the things which I have yet to begin.

2. To understand that my progress is not a performance and that I am not going to be perfect in all I do, but I am going to continue moving forward in a consistent direction with the Lord.

3. To understand that my thoughts and imaginations are powerful tools from God that help me create the future I want. My life in the days ahead will be the sum total of my choices from days past. If I am to go farther than I first thought possible, I will have to go beyond where I have stopped to reach the end.

4. I will remember that process and preparation are a vital part of my forward progress. As an athlete has to stretch before he runs his race, I recognize that after I make the solid commitment to move forward with God, I will need to be stretched and prepared for that new growth. I will not be afraid to go through this process as often as necessary, because I want to live my life to its full potential.

5. My focus to move forward must be greater than my desire for comfort and ease. I will not sabotage my own progress in the things

of the Lord. When I find myself off track, I will repent and get back in alignment with the purposes I believe God has planned for me.

Just as we spoke about embracing our vision and developing corresponding actions for our vision, these five statements of review can be used for that purpose; they are action statements. They declare what you will do as you continue to move forward. Refer back to them as often as you need to.

As we enter Section II, we will turn our focus to hearing. I will still challenge you to make confessions of faith and to take corresponding actions based on what you read at the conclusion of each chapter. However, I might not steer you quite as directly as I did in Section I. Now that we are building some forward momentum, you will need to stoke the fire and keep it hot for yourself.

Hearing from God is something that takes practice and certainly has a learning curve, so just as we focused on moving forward and not giving up in Section I, we will now have an opportunity to focus on our determination and commitment to hear from God and grow in our walk with the Lord. Hearing from God comes primarily in three ways:

1. The inward witness, a gentle leading in your own spirit.

2. The still small voice of your spirit, which has received from the Holy Spirit.

3. The voice of the Holy Spirit within, which is usually much more authoritative.

We will discuss these more at the end of Section II.

Section II: Hearing

Chapter 6: Are You the One?

There is therefore now no condemnation to those who are
in Christ Jesus, who do not walk according to the flesh, but
according to the Spirit.
—Romans 8:1

In this chapter, we will be looking at one of two scriptural observations that are contained in Section II. Although it is not a parable, it does address an important issue we will all face at some point in our lives. This section begins with an emphasis on hearing because I believe the Lord wants to challenge us in a much deeper way than in Section I, which was about developing the determination to grow and become more committed to your personal walk with the Lord. Section II takes us a step further, and is more about what is taking place inwardly (in your heart and spirit) than what is taking place outwardly as demonstrated by the corresponding actions you were encouraged to engage in while reading the parables in Section I.

The two portions of Scripture contained in this chapter are about doubt and questioning, which in and of themselves are not always bad. Questioning, much like need, is the prevailing force to the discovery or creation of most inventions and is the catalyst of our convictions. It is healthy to question things, for if we just went along with the status quo all the time, how would we ever achieve change or make progress? Healthy questioning is good for the soul!

Before we really explore what I just said, let me explain a few things. First, God is never the author of doubt in our lives, even though it is inevitable that we will all experience this condition at times. Doubt is the work of Satan and is meant to bring fear and confusion to us and to draw us away from the Lord. God is fully aware of Satan's devices and strategies and is not moved by him or his tactics. God is faithful to reveal these things to us as His children so we won't be moved either.

Additionally, questioning has both a healthy and positive aspect—which leads to discovery, or the revealing of something once hidden—and a negative aspect which leads to doubt, fear, confusion, and the questioning of our own abilities or worse, the Lord's. Many times in my life I have found that when God wants to reveal something to me He asks me a question. Questioning in this sense causes me to search, and this type of searching usually brings an answer or understanding to a thing or issue I may not have learned or discovered in any other way.

The conditions of doubt and fear are part of the negative aspects of questioning, and more often than not they bring confusion. Questioning, in this sense, must be answered with what the Bible says. If these conditions are left unchallenged, these thoughts and emotions can lead to a hardening of the heart and destroy your faith. However, when these issues are confronted with the truth, they will lead to a hardening of your beliefs, and become your rock-solid convictions!

"Who am I, and what am I here for?" is the universal question. Satan will lie to you, saying that you're a loser, a victim, a hypocrite, or the one person God's promises just won't work for. Satan's intention is to destroy your faith by capitalizing on how he can make you feel.

The Holy Spirit tells you the truth—you are forgiven, a new creation in Christ, a joint-heir with Christ, more than a conqueror through Christ who loves you, an overcomer, and a born-again child of God who is a believer carrying God's authority. These truths build your faith and have nothing to do with how you feel; God wants us to act according to our restored position in Christ rather than the temporary conditions we might be experiencing at any given time.

Read these two portions of Scripture and see how Jesus addressed the issue of doubt and questioning. Recognize how Jesus deals with John the Baptist concerning his position in the kingdom of God rather than his own temporary condition.

> The next day John saw Jesus coming toward him, and said, "Behold! The Lamb of God who takes away the sin

of the world! This is He of whom I said, 'After me comes a Man who is preferred before me, for He was before me.' I did not know Him; but that He should be revealed to Israel, therefore I came baptizing with water." And John bore witness, saying, "I saw the Spirit descending from heaven like a dove, and He remained upon Him. I did not know Him, but He who sent me to baptize with water said to me, 'Upon whom you see the Spirit descending, and remaining on Him, this is He who baptizes with the Holy Spirit.' And I have seen and testified that this is the Son of God" (John 1:29-34).

A short time later, and after John the Baptist was imprisoned for calling Herod out over the sin of taking his brother's wife, we again pick up our story.

When Jesus had finished giving these instructions to his twelve disciples, he went out to teach and preach in towns throughout the region. John the Baptist, who was in prison, heard about all the things the Messiah was doing. So he sent his disciples to ask Jesus, "Are you the Messiah we've been expecting, or should we keep looking for someone else?" Jesus told them, "Go back to John and tell him what you have heard and seen—the blind see, the lame walk, the lepers are cured, the deaf hear, the dead are raised to life, and the Good News is being preached to the poor. And tell him, 'God blesses those who do not turn away because of me.'"

As John's disciples were leaving, Jesus began talking about him to the crowds. "What kind of man did you go into the wilderness to see? Was he a weak reed, swayed by every breath of wind? Or were you expecting to see a man dressed in expensive clothes? No, people with expensive clothes live in palaces. Were you looking for a prophet? Yes, and he is more than a prophet. John is the man to whom the Scriptures refer when they say, 'Look,

I am sending my messenger ahead of you, and he will prepare your way before you.'

"I tell you the truth, of all who have ever lived, none is greater than John the Baptist. Yet even the least person in the Kingdom of Heaven is greater than he is! (Matthew 11:1-11 NLT).

John was called by God to "prepare the way of the Lord," a voice crying in the wilderness so that all flesh would see the salvation of God. John's calling was set in place before his birth and was revealed by an angel to his father, Zacharias, while he served his duty in the temple. Luke 1 reveals these details along with those of Jesus' birth and how John and Jesus were entwined even before their births. It's worth reading before you continue.

As we fast-forward about thirty years, Scripture records that John spent years alone in the wilderness being prepared for his calling; when the time was right, he appeared out of the wilderness, preaching repentance of sin and baptizing with water. It was also at this time that Jesus and John come face to face with each other for the first time. Matthew lets us in on their conversation as they stood there together in the waters of the Jordan:

Then Jesus went from Galilee to the Jordan River to be baptized by John. But John tried to talk him out of it. "I am the one who needs to be baptized by you," he said, "so why are you coming to me?" But Jesus said, "It should be done, for we must carry out all that God requires." So John agreed to baptize him (Matthew 3:13-15 NLT).

As a former children's pastor, from time to time I took what I called "scriptural liberties" to help get a point across to the children. To get the kids to jump into the pages of their Bibles and use their five senses when we read. We actually would stand up and jump forward to symbolize this. I wanted them to feel the heat of the sun, smell the smoke of the sacrifices burning on the altar, hear the noise of the crowds in the temple, and so on. Most importantly, I wanted them to see the men and women of the Bible for who they were.

Many times, we read the Bible as if we were reading a fictitious story and then wonder why we struggle to have faith in a God we can't see. The Bible is both spiritually and historically accurate, and every single person mentioned in Scripture lived and breathed here on earth as we do today. The events recorded throughout the Bible are most assuredly supernatural, but they occurred in the lives of very natural, ordinary people like you and me. This is what is revealed in the latter half of our Scripture text above.

Yes, John said, "And I have seen and testified that this is the Son of God" (John 1:34). Immediately after, he baptized Jesus and heard the voice from heaven declare, "…This is My beloved Son, in whom I am well pleased" (Matthew 3:17). But now John sits in the depths of Herod's prison, alone and emotionally empty, his isolation prompting him to question even those things that he declared as absolute truth just months earlier.

With plenty of time to think and having his very convictions challenged by the thoughts bombarding his mind, John struggled and began to have doubts. This confusion brought about the questioning that eventually led him to send his own disciples to ask Jesus, "Are you the One, or do we seek another?"

Charles Finney was a great man of God and is known for starting several great revivals, including one here in the town where I live. Early in the nineteenth century, he made the following observation: "The theaters are full because the world lies well and the churches are empty because the church tells the truth poorly." Doubt concerning the things of the Lord wasn't the culprit here; the truth being told poorly was. It did not feed or satisfy the hunger of the soul in need, and doubt was able to grow from a state of questioning to one of hardening the heart. Again the best way to combat doubt, confusion, and questioning is to feed on the truth. Let's see how Jesus did that with John the Baptist.

While standing in the Jordan, Jesus convinced John that God's will needed to be fulfilled by John baptizing Jesus. He knew that John had witnessed the Holy Spirit descending on Him and heard the voice of His Father declare, "This is My Son." The triune God was in full manifestation right before John's very eyes, and yet Jesus' response was not disgust or condemnation because of the questioning in John's heart, but compassion and understanding.

Re-read Matthew 11. Jesus said to John's disciples, "Go back to John and tell him what you have heard and seen—the blind see, the lame walk, the lepers are cured, the deaf hear, the dead are raised to life, and the Good News is being preached to the poor. And tell him, 'God blesses those who do not turn away because of me.'" (Matthew 11:4-6 NLT).

Here is one of those times that we jump into our Bibles. Matthew continues: "As John's disciples were leaving, Jesus began talking about him to the crowds (Matthew 11:7 NLT). Stop with me and see what is taking place. Look around at the crowds. Look—there are John's disciples. Imagine with me—as John's disciples are walking away, they hear Jesus begin to speak about John, and they pause and listen with great anticipation. Can you see them? Look at the joy they receive in their own hearts as Jesus confirms to the crowds that John is the greatest of all prophets!

Imagine with me as they return to John in the prison, isolated and alone, struggling with his own thoughts and purpose. Imagine his anticipation to hear the report sent back to him by Jesus and then to hear his own disciples tell of how Jesus praised John for his work in "preparing the way of the Lord" before the crowds. Wow!

This retelling of John's purpose by Jesus and relayed by John's own disciples had to cause John to recall all that had taken place, what he had seen, what he had heard, and most of all what God had told him about these events before they even occurred. John's resolve and convictions had to be strengthened and solidified beyond question. Jesus had answered John's doubt properly with the truth. John said before his imprisonment that Jesus must increase, and he must decrease (John 3:30). I am sure the message sent back by Jesus renewed John's understanding of his purpose and strengthened his ability to continue.

How does this apply to us today? We all have times when we struggle with doubt and questioning, but we must do as John did: "Go and ask Jesus." John had to send his disciples to ask Jesus, but we have the ability to go directly to Him in prayer and ask Him ourselves. And we have His word in Scripture to confirm what we hear.

Just as Jesus sent back word to strengthen John's faith and resolve rather than a sharp word of condemnation or disgust in his struggle, He is ready to do the same for us whenever we call out to Him for help. Here is an opportunity to feed our faith. Do not listen to the lies that God won't or can't help you. Instead, listen to Hebrews:

> Seeing then that we have a great High Priest who has passed through the heavens, Jesus the Son of God, let us hold fast our confession. For we do not have a High Priest who cannot sympathize with our weaknesses, but was in all points tempted as we are, yet without sin. Let us therefore come boldly to the throne of grace, that we may obtain mercy and find grace to help in time of need (Hebrews 4:14-16).

God will help us and wants to help us! Peter walking on the water is yet another example of how Jesus is there to help us overcome our doubts and even the fear that sometimes comes with them:

> "Then Peter called to him, "Lord, if it's really you, tell me to come to you, walking on the water." "Yes, come," Jesus said. So Peter went over the side of the boat and walked on the water toward Jesus. But when he saw the strong wind and the waves, he was terrified and began to sink. "Save me, Lord!" he shouted. Jesus *immediately* reached out and grabbed him. "You have so little faith," Jesus said. *"Why did you doubt me?"* When they climbed back into the boat, the wind stopped. Then the disciples worshiped him. "You really are the Son of God!" they exclaimed (Matthew 14:28-33 NLT).

Listen to what Jesus said and also *how* He said it: "Peter, you were already walking on the water. You mastered the wind and waves. Why did you doubt Me?" And look not only at what Jesus said, but how He responded to Peter's need—*immediately*. Jesus reached out His hand and caught him! Do we really think He would do any less for us? We are His beloved, His purpose and His passion.

Consider the Squirrel

When we find ourselves doubting God or facing some type of trial, test, or struggle, we need to remember that these things are not always an indication that we are doing something wrong or that we are out of the will of God. John wasn't in any willful sin, but he was isolated from the fellowship of those who could keep him encouraged and built up in his faith. Peter was walking atop the waves in a tremendous act of faith and by the presence of circumstances became fearful, took his eyes off Jesus for a moment, and began to sink.

As a final word of encouragement to you in this chapter, consider with me the apostle Paul who was the most persecuted man of the Bible. He was stoned, beaten, jailed, shipwrecked, and in a tempest at sea a night and a day. Let's see what he has to say about doubt:

> For I am persuaded *beyond doubt* (am sure) that neither death nor life, nor angels nor principalities, nor things impending and threatening nor things to come, nor powers, nor height nor depth, nor anything else in all creation will be able to separate us from the love of God which is in Christ Jesus our Lord (Romans 8:38-39 AMP).

Paul did not say he didn't experience doubt. What he is saying is that even in the presence of doubt, he looked beyond it to the truth and drew his strength from what God said and promised, and we must do the same.

If and when you are struggling with doubt, confusion, or questioning, feed on the truth of God's Word. Read and re-read this chapter. Keep God's perspective on the issue. Search the Scriptures for the promises of God that combat the lies you are being bombarded with and believe what Paul declared. *Beyond doubt—nothing shall separate us from the love of God!*

Faith Declaration: For the word of God is living and powerful and sharper than any two-edged sword, piercing even to the division of soul (what I think) and spirit (what God's Word says). I will not be moved by what I see or feel, but will learn to become persuaded beyond doubt and trust in the love of God in all things!

Chapter 7: Don't Let Go, Daddy

And you, fathers, do not provoke your children to wrath, but
bring them up in the training and admonition of the Lord.
—Ephesians 6:4

There we were at the playground, out in the grassy field with the slightly downward slope. I had finally convinced my daughter, Marla, that she could ride her bike without her training wheels. Very reluctantly, she agreed, but only if I would hold on to her bike as she rode, to which I also agreed. With that, her day of reckoning had finally come. Marla had a pretty fancy bike for back in her day. It had a banana seat with a little sissy bar and tassels hanging off its handle bars, and of course, her shiny new helmet.

So as agreed, here was our plan: She was going to pedal down that slope, and I was going to run next to her and hold onto her sissy bar to keep her bike upright. The first few trips went surprisingly smooth in both of our estimations, so naturally this built her confidence and she was willing to keep up this routine.

Now that you can imagine this scenario, let me tell you what else was happening. With each pass, Marla became more stable, even though she was pedaling through the grass, and as she rode she was shouting, "Don't let go, Daddy!" almost continually.

I repeatedly answered, "Okay, honey. Just keep going!" But while I was running beside her, I began to loosen my grip and eventually was just holding my hand out flat over her sissy bar as she rode and I ran.

Now of course, Marla had no idea I was doing this, and all would have been fine if I had just kept this as my little secret. But no, that was wisdom far beyond my level of understanding at the time. So the next time down the hill, we started out as usual, and after I got her going I stopped to watch as any proud Dad would do. Yep, you guessed it! As soon as she saw I was gone, she toppled, and then she let me know in very certain terms that this was unacceptable and she was done!

Now fast-forward with me ten years. It's not the bike anymore; it's the car. And it's not the playground anymore; it's the school dance. Things weren't really going all that well for Marla because, as our oldest daughter, she also served as the guinea pig for her three siblings. We were at an impasse in our communications, for sure. Things weren't as easy as "Do it because I said so" anymore; teenagers aren't so easily convinced to do what you say.

As I sat in church one Sunday morning during this season in our lives, we had a guest minister preaching about flying his plane by instruments alone and not by looking out at the horizon. As he drew the parallel of how similar this was to walking by faith and not by sight, I drifted.

I was daydreaming and thinking about our struggles with my daughter when God said to me, "Remember when Marla was six years old and you were teaching her how to ride her bike? Your job then was to let go while she thought you were holding on, and now you have to hold on while she thinks you have let go."

When God spoke this to me, I'll admit I answered back kind of sarcastically with, "That was easy when she was six, Father!" Yeah, I was feeling a little sorry for myself. But God doesn't let up when He has a point to make, and He knew better than I did about what I needed to do. I'd love to tell you in perfect Pollyanna Christian fashion how everything was fine after that, but that wasn't always the case. Sometimes I can be a little thickheaded, and it took years to realize that God wasn't telling me how to deal with Marla that Sunday morning, but how to deal with myself.

This was about my ability to lead in accordance with how the Holy Spirit leads us in a still, small voice, meaning He doesn't need to manipulate or coerce. I wasn't learning and growing in my ability to lead as quickly as my daughter was growing in her need for good leadership. I had not adapted or even realized my need to change yet from "Do it because I told you to do it" to taking the necessary time to teach and equip her to make good choices for herself without fear.

My pastor, John Carter of Abundant Life Christian Center in Syracuse, New York, shared with us the Hebrew word *akareeth,* which means to consider the end of a thing or consider what results this will bring. This is what God was saying to me about Marla when He said, "Now you must hold on while she thinks you have let go." He meant, "Teach her to make for herself the kind of decisions you want her to make by teaching her to consider the outcome before she makes them."

This was a stark contrast to the "do it because I told you to" method, or even worse yet, making her feel coerced or manipulated into doing something. That is far more likely to result in rebellion and is exactly what I was causing to take place in my daughter at the time. I was feeding her rebellion by starving her need for the answers and growth that were proper for her development and maturity as a sixteen-year-old.

Unlike my own leadership skills at a critical time in my daughter's development, God is fully equipped and able to lead us into a greater understanding and maturity in all things that pertain to this life. How often do you imagine He has orchestrated circumstances on our behalf so we could make the choices necessary to experience the abundant life He intended, or so we could see and recognize His efforts to bring us into maturity? God certainly knows what He is trying to do in our lives, and if we cooperate, look at what we could have: "For I know the thoughts and plans that I have for you, says the Lord, thoughts and plans for welfare and peace and not for evil, to give you hope in your final outcome" (Jeremiah 29:11 AMP).

I have learned and am still learning to consider the outcome of my choices before I make them, and at times I still have to go back and change things or stop things because I acted too quickly or before I had fully considered a thing in light of God's ultimate plan for me.

No doubt, friend, God is always holding on to us, especially during the times when we think He's let go. And just as I was there for Marla and would have held her upright if she had begun to tip over on her bike, God will do the same for us. It's in His plans.

Consider the Squirrel

That's not to say you and I never will fall. But even when that happens, I am certain God will be there to pick us up and brush us off for another attempt. These are the days when we must learn to follow well, so that at other stages in our lives we will be able to lead just as well.

Why not take some time and discuss with Him the limitless wisdom He displays on our behalf every day, knowing He has a plan for our lives, and shout out to Him: "Don't let go, Daddy!" to which He might reply, *"Okay, my child. Just keep going!"*

Faith Declaration: I believe God has a plan for me and trust that He is upholding me by His mighty hand. I am determined to consider the end of a thing before I make any decisions. God's plan is to give me peace and hope in my final outcome, therefore I trust Him to lead me and declare I will follow His plans for my life.

Chapter 8: The Two-Dollar Chicken Pot Pie

Whoever shuts his ears to the cry of the poor will also cry himself and not be heard.
—Proverbs 21:13

For God so loved the world that He gave His only begotten Son, that whoever believes in Him should not perish but have everlasting life.
—John 3:16

Off to the grocery store on Christmas Eve morning—yeah, that's just what I wanted to do. But we already had most of our shopping done, so picking up a few forgotten items wouldn't be all that eventful, or so I thought.

Turns out I was wrong, but as you will soon see, it was for a great reason. As I got into the store and grabbed my cart, it dawned on me as I reached into my back pocket that I had forgotten my wallet. Well, I abandoned my cart and headed back to the house, which is only a mile or so from the store.

On my way back home, I noticed a woman walking along the opposite side of the road. She had a hood pulled over her head and was struggling to carry what looked like a duffle bag across her shoulders. It was cold and snowing and the wind was blowing. It was not nice out.

My wife, Lisa, had gone for a run on the snowmobile trails behind the house and wasn't home while I made my quick turnaround. After grabbing my wallet, I headed back down the road to the store. And there she was again—the same woman with the hood, just a little farther along the way, but now on my side of the road.

As I came up closer to her, I got this overwhelming feeling that I was supposed to do something for her. I passed by her slowly and said, "God, was I supposed to pick her up?" I even looked for a place to turn around. There really wasn't any place to do so until the actual entrance of the shopping center, and by then the unction to do something seemed to subside.

I prayed, "Lord, if I was supposed to pick her up and help her, teach me how to be more sensitive to Your Spirit so I won't miss You when You want me to do something unusual." I didn't really sense anything further, so I parked and went back into the store.

As I went about the store, picking up the few items on Lisa's list, I ran into several people I knew, and after the customary Merry Christmas small talk, I made my way to the front of the store to check out. Now, there are about fifteen to twenty checkout lanes in the store, and as I looked for a short line, I made a quick decision and dipped into a line only to look up and see the woman from the road again, checking out right in front of me.

It was just the two of us in line, and she was purchasing nothing but a two-dollar pot pie with the receipts she had from redeeming deposits on bottles and cans. I stood there in shock that here she was again, and after I realized what she was doing, I heard God tell me to give her twenty dollars.

She finished up and walked out with her empty duffle bag in hand. I quickly paid for my groceries with my debit card so I could get a twenty-dollar bill back and immediately headed out the door to find her. But she was gone. I looked all around, thinking to myself, "She's on foot; how far could she get?"

I eventually walked to my car in frustration, and as I opened up the trunk to put my two bags in, the thought came to me, "Oh well, it's the thought that counts." I immediately shot back aloud, "No, that won't feed or help anybody. I need to find her!"

I got in the car and cruised to the front of the store area one more time. To my relief, there she was picking up half-smoked cigarettes by a butt can. I pulled up in the loading zone and quickly got out of my car. As I walked toward her, she noticed me coming and seemed to be afraid, as if she thought she was in trouble.

As I approached her, she walked back over next to a shopping cart, which held her empty duffle bag in the child seat with her pot pie lying on top of it. I smiled at her and asked, "Hey, can I talk to you for a minute?"

She never said a word to me, but did make eye contact as I put my hand on her shoulder. As we stood there, I explained how God had pointed her out to me while she was walking to the grocery store, and then I said to her, "The Lord wanted me to let you know He knows right where you are, and what you are going through right now. He wanted me to let you know the Lord Jesus Christ loves you very much, and He wanted me to give this to you." I handed her the folded twenty dollar bill; she definitely could see what it was, and then looked up at me, still without saying a word. I said, "It's okay. God just wanted to let you know He loves you." We just looked at each other for another moment; she never did speak to me.

As I removed my hand from her shoulder, I kind of just patted her shoulder a couple of times as she stared at that folded bill, then tucked it into her coat pocket as we walked away from each other.

When I got back into my car, I just broke down in tears. I had just represented my Father again, and His love overwhelmed me. As I said, it was only a mile or so to home, and as I walked in the door, Lisa, now back from her run, could see on my face something had happened to me while I was out. She asked, "You okay?" As I told her what had just happened, her face began to change, and she seemed overwhelmed as well.

She said, "I saw that same woman as I looked out the window while I was getting ready for my run. I thought to myself, *God, should I go pick her up and take her to where she's going?* I realized the jeep was out of gas and knew if I went to get gas and came back, she might be gone. Then I thought, *Oh well. It's the thought that counts.* But I said aloud, 'No, that won't help her,' so I prayed, *Lord make her stand out to Bobby as he is coming home from the store and have him help her.*"

Consider the Squirrel

So there we both stood, grocery bags at my feet, realizing the depth of what had just taken place. God had used us both and had spoken to both of us in a significant way. We both even had the same thought and had refused to accept it, and we refused it aloud. We both were spurred to action and now, just for a few moments, stood there and pondered how amazing what had just happened was for us—and for the woman with the two-dollar pot pie.

There is so much that I could go into here about how God answers prayer, hearing from the Holy Spirit, God's love for us, and the lengths He will go to reach us—or even how it truly is more blessed to give than receive.

First, let me tell you that at the time this took place, my own family was in the middle of an intense struggle. I had lost my job months earlier, and we were standing in faith for many breakthroughs for ourselves.

What God did through us that day for this woman was every bit as much for us as it was for her. I realized later, as I was retelling the story at our Christmas dinner table, that what the Lord had me say to her was really what He had been trying to get across to us. He knew right where we were and what we were going through. He wanted us to know that He loved us and wasn't going to let us fail.

The first significant thing to consider here is that when we go through personal times of struggle we tend to focus first on what is going on around us—how we feel, what we think, what we're going to do. Until we have developed a steadfast trust in God's Word, we tend not to consider or focus enough on what's going on *inside* us, meaning what is happening spiritually rather than outwardly or circumstantially.

Through this time of struggle, Lisa and I continued on our own journey of learning how to stop doing and how to become more Spirit-focused first. I won't say we have it down pat, but we consider what's going on inside us and around us spiritually more so now than we ever did over the first twenty-five years of our Christian walk.

Until this time of struggle in our lives, we believed we could pray away or faith away our troubles and just ignored that this was a really hit-or-miss approach. We actually made excuses for why things didn't work out or, worse yet, why God didn't come through for us. Sound familiar? We even toed the old religious line of, "Well, I am sure God can do it, so there must be something we are doing wrong that kept this from working." It's my experience that a vast majority of Christians live with this jaded mentality, which is not at all how God wants things to be.

It's true that God is our deliverer, but His greater blessing for us is that we become overcomers and conquerors rather than always being the rescued! God is not the initiator of our struggles, but He certainly wants to see us triumph in them, and He uses every opportunity to strengthen us so we can defeat the strategies and thwart Satan's plans against us.

Before you get riled up about what I said about prayer or faith, let me explain more fully. We need to pray, and we most definitely need to use our faith, but having weapons and not using them properly makes them of little use against a master of arms. The Devil is very cunning and crafty as well as a deceptive enemy, and if he can discourage us or make our faith seem of no effect, we oftentimes will give up, even though we are the more dominant opponent in any struggle against him. "He who is in you is greater than he who is in the world" (1 John 4:4).

On an actual battle field, there are spotters on the ground called *forward observers* as well as those who actually deliver the ordinances or bombs. The forward observers see what targets need to be destroyed and relay their exact positions to those who will drop bombs or shoot and destroy those given targets.

The Holy Spirit is our Forward Observer in times of struggle, and although we possess a great arsenal of weapons, without His pinpoint accuracy and timing, all that we possess will be of little consequence in our struggles. This really exposes a major lack in the lives of most Christians today: We rarely rely on the Holy Spirit above our own natural wisdom, or even what we alone have gleaned from the Scriptures.

So again, the first significant thing we learned during this time of difficulty in our lives was how little we had been relying on the leading of the Holy Spirit and how to give Him first place in our decisions and plans. Jesus, speaking about the Holy Spirit said: "When the Spirit of truth comes, he will *guide you* into all truth. He will not speak on his own but will *tell you* what he has heard. He will *tell you* about the future.

Consider the Squirrel

He will bring me glory by *telling you* whatever he receives from me."
(John 16:13-14 NLT).

We have to learn to walk in all that belongs to us once we have received
Jesus Christ as our Lord. The apostle Paul was a religious teacher of the
law and walked in all the understanding he had concerning the Scriptures,
but he learned after his conversion how little he really understood them
without the revelation the Holy Spirit could bring to them.

Just as Paul came to realize how deeply impacting the spirit world
was on what he perceived as everyday life, we need to do the same. I'm
not talking about some spooky spiritual nonsense here, or that there is a
devil behind every tree or under every rock, but I am saying heaven and
hell and the occupants of the spirit realm are more real than what we can
perceive with our natural minds only.

I know it is a natural tendency for most folks to dismiss things they
don't fully comprehend as "not important," but we can't afford to do this
concerning the things of God. God is a Spirit, and people, created in His
image, can be no less. Mankind is an eternal spirit who has a soul and
lives in a body, and one day, when these bodies will no longer sustain
our lives in this realm, we will not cease to exist except in this natural
realm; our spirits will live on.

The Bible contains many promises from God to us, but we still must
learn to be led by His Holy Spirit on what, when, and how to appropriate
those promises on our behalf and gain and sustain victory over the
struggles of our everyday lives.

The second thing that was significant to us that we discovered during
this Christmas Eve was how easy it was to actually hear the Holy Spirit
once we recognized how He spoke to us. Back on the review page for
Section I, I wrote about the three ways God generally speaks to us—first
and primarily through an inward witness, which is just a confirming
sense of knowing from within. This is what happened to me when I saw
the woman on the side of the road; I had a sense that I was supposed
to do something for her. Second is the voice of our spirit, which also
originates from within, and third is the voice of the Holy Spirit, which is
also from within but is recognized as much more authoritative than the
voice of our own spirit.

The more we learn to flow with these leadings in the Spirit, the more accurate, confident, and comfortable we become with them. In the same way you learn to recognize the voice of a caller on your phone, you can learn to recognize these three leadings of the Holy Spirit. It was comfortable for me to give a twenty dollar bill to this woman because what I heard in my spirit lined up with what I could see in the natural—she was in need. But what if God had told me to do the same for a man in front of me wearing a three-piece suit?

My comfort level would have been much more challenged because I would have been going only on what I heard. But the Holy Spirit, knowing what we couldn't possibly know by outward or natural circumstances, might have been aware that this guy's wife just got diagnosed with breast cancer and earlier that day he had cried out, "God, if You're real and You can hear me, please show me You're there."

With that information, approaching him just the same way I did that woman wouldn't seem strange at all. It actually would be quite amazing and awesome to be a part of that. Imagine approaching him and saying exactly what I said to the woman: "The Lord wanted me to let you know that He knows right where you are and what you are going through right now. He wanted me to let you know the Lord Jesus Christ loves you very much and wanted me to give this to you." That twenty bucks in his hands would have become the object of faith that reminded him that God showed up in a tangible way to indeed say, "Yes, I AM real, and I AM here for you!"

The only thing keeping these types of things from happening more often isn't the lack of great need in our society, but the lack of those who have chosen to become great hearers and doers of the Word. This is why we must learn to function in accordance with the leadings of God, and specifically the One who Jesus sent to help us in this life—our Comforter, the Holy Spirit.

If I relied only on my own understanding when I heard in my spirit, *Give him twenty dollars*, I would end up looking at his suit and the circumstances that I could see with my natural understanding and dismiss the idea as ridiculous or because of my fear of looking stupid. Then because of my own inability to hear or my refusal to obey the One

Consider the Squirrel

I profess to know, this man would have gone away in unnecessary grief and despair with no idea God was trying to reach out to him.

This small example is relatable enough for us all to understand how limited we live most of our lives and how much more of God is available for us all. The depth of understanding of all that God has and is doing for us as His children is so much greater than I could possibly attempt to cover or reveal in this book, but to stay on point concerning the things we experience in our daily lives here and now, I needed to explain just this small portion of information.

God is for us when all is going well, when it is not, and even when we open the door to our own troubles at times. But every difficulty we face might not be the outcome of some sin or error we have walked in. Sometimes it might just be a heartless menacing act of the god of this world, which is what Second Corinthians 4:4 calls Satan. Yet regardless of their origin, one thing remains completely true and unchanging when we face the trials of this life: The more we learn to rely on the Holy Spirit and the more we learn to trust the promises found in Scripture, the more victory and peace we will walk in, even in the midst of our difficulties.

Lisa and I received great hope that Christmas Eve through all that took place that day, and also through what we came to realize about our own struggles later during times of prayer and contemplation before the Lord. I'm so thankful that we didn't ignore the inward witness we both received that Christmas Eve morning. It has helped us to have more peace now than we can possibly explain.

Faith Declaration: I am a spirit who has a soul and lives in a body. This truth demands that I rely on the Holy Spirit for wisdom and revelation even while I read Scripture. I will not forget that He will lead me into all truth and show me things to come, and so I declare I trust the Holy Spirit, for I remember greater is He who is in me than he who is in the world.

Chapter 9: "I Saw Your Baby Girl. She's Perfect."

*There is so much more I want to tell you, but you can't bear it now. When the Spirit of truth comes, he will guide you into all truth. He will not speak on his own but will tell you what he has heard. **He will tell you about the future.** He will bring me glory by telling you whatever he receives from me. All that belongs to the Father is mine; this is why I said, "The Spirit will tell you whatever he receives from me."*
—John 16:12-15 NLT

You know, some folks have all kinds of opinions and ideas about the prophetic nature of God, and although it might make for plenty of conversation, the only opinion that really matters on this subject is God's. The Scripture above is what God has to say about His own prophetic nature as well as a few things about the Holy Spirit.

Jesus was talking to His disciples in the upper room and revealing to them that the time had come to fulfill His ultimate mission. He knew there were many things that they needed to know, but they would not be able to understand them until after Holy Spirit came and they were born again.

Twenty-some years ago my wife, Lisa, and I were at church with our six-year-old daughter, Marla, and our three-year-old son, Aaron. We were doing the whole after-church fellowship thing when a friend of ours approached Lisa and said, "I had a dream about y'all the other night."

We stood there and listened to Mary share with us what God had spoken to her in a dream concerning Lisa and I, and most specifically our baby girl; the interesting thing was we didn't have a baby girl and we weren't planning on having any more children.

Now when it comes to the gifts of the Spirit and their operation in our lives today, people tend to have all kinds of reactions and ideas—mainly based on how they've been taught or because of their religious affiliations—but the Bible needs to be our only trusted source of information on these matters. The Bible very plainly speaks about the nine gifts of the Holy Spirit.

> But the manifestation of the Spirit is given to each one for the profit of all: for to one is given the word of wisdom through the Spirit, to another the word of knowledge through the same Spirit, to another faith by the same Spirit, to another gifts of healings by the same Spirit, to another the working of miracles, to another prophecy, to another discerning of spirits, to another different kinds of tongues, to another the interpretation of tongues. But one and the same Spirit works all these things, distributing to each one individually as He wills (1 Corinthians 12:7-11).

What Mary was sharing with Lisa and me that afternoon would be classified as a word of wisdom, which was a portion of the wisdom of God that dealt with the will and purposes of God concerning a future event. There was just one problem though: Lisa and I hadn't heard anything at all from God about any more children, nor did we want any more at the time.

Kenneth E. Hagin, who is probably the best author and teacher I have ever read concerning the gifts of the Spirit, explains in one of his books what to do in a situation like ours. Since we had just recently graduated from Bible college, his instructions still were fresh in my mind when Mary spoke to us. Any time you are given a prophetic word, it should confirm something you already have in your heart. At the very least, it should bring clarity to what you might have been tossing around in your own thoughts.

If it doesn't confirm something, seems like the first you've heard of it, or you haven't yet considered the thing, Brother Hagin says, "Shelve it." What he means is that you should store it away—don't act on it or run off and begin some new thing just because somebody else said they've heard from God about you—and that's exactly what we did.

We told our friend that was very interesting, but didn't see how that applied to us since we didn't have a baby girl and weren't even planning on having any more children. This took place around 1988. Lisa and I eventually did want another child and prayed and planned for what became the birth of our son, Timothy, in April of 1990.

After Timothy was born, Lisa and I actually talked about the "word" Mary had shared with us and dismissed it as, well, sometimes we just miss the things of the Spirit, and we went about our lives. However, two years later our daughter, Emily, was born with a heart condition, and it was then that we were reminded of and needed the "word" we had been given by Mary.

Remember, a word of wisdom is a portion of the wisdom of God that deals with the will and purposes of God concerning a future event. Just because it didn't make any sense to us at the time didn't mean God wasn't aware of what would become a reality in our lives later.

We would lay our hands on Emily and speak over her what God had said through Mary as a provision for us years earlier. We reminded Father God what Mary had spoken to us: "I saw your baby girl; she's perfect, strong, and healthy in every way!" We would thank God for the promise He had given us long before we knew we needed it, and now we had peace knowing He was fully aware—years before her birth—that we would need His words of encouragement and exhortation to comfort us.

Remember the words of Jesus in our Scripture text for this chapter: "[The Spirit of truth] will bring me glory *by telling you whatever he receives from me.* All that belongs to the Father is mine; this is why I said, "The Spirit will tell you whatever he receives from me" (John 16:15 NLT). We believed this passage and held God to what we believed He had said to us through Mary.

God is the God of all things seen and unseen, known and unknown by humans. His wisdom transcends our ability to fully comprehend.

Scripture says that although we see dimly now, we will one day see and know all things (1 Corinthians 13:12). Until then, we must learn to rely on God's Word and the Holy Spirit to reveal to us the ways of God that we need to know for now.

The ways of the Spirit are an uncomfortable topic for many people and dismissed by others as the mysteries of God or, worse yet, no longer in operation or needed, but the Bible clearly does not teach any of those unscriptural beliefs. It wouldn't be logical to acknowledge that the Holy Spirit is here to bring us into the knowledge of salvation without also bringing us into the knowledge of the ways of the kingdom. The supernatural ability of Father God to express Himself to us through the gifts of the Spirit and His Word is just as necessary today as in the days and years after Christ's resurrection.

Lisa and I can say today that our daughter is completely perfect in every way, and she has no side effects or symptoms of her past ailments; it's not even something we consider except in testimony now. God is good, and His mercy endures forever. His Word is eternal, His abilities are unlimited, and His love for us is without measure; however, the Bible says that Jesus could do no mighty works in His own hometown because of the unbelief there. All He is and can do on our behalf must be received and operated in our lives today by faith.

You will find many places in the Gospels where Jesus simply tells folks, "Only believe," which connotes that He will do the rest! If some of the truths I have shared in this chapter are new to you or are different than the traditions you grew up with, then pray without limitations and ask the Holy Spirit to reveal Himself to you in a fresh and new way.

He is faithful and will not withhold Himself from you. Remember, the truth you know and understand concerning God's Word is what sets you free.

Faith Declaration: God is a Spirit and must be worshiped in the Spirit. I am a spirit who has a soul and lives in a body; therefore I can and will worship God in the Spirit. His truths are what set me free and give me the ability to believe His promises.

Chapter 10: Perception: Hearing Is the Beginning of Believing

So faith comes from hearing, that is, hearing the Good News about Christ.
—Romans 10:17 NLT

For indeed the gospel was preached to us as well as to them; but the word which they heard did not profit them, not being mixed with faith in those who heard it.
—Hebrews 4:2

Perception, some say, is reality; this means that whatever you believe to be true is true to you, regardless of whether it's true at all. We don't usually see things as they are; we see things as *we are*. This is why several people can hear or see the same thing and then recall several different versions of the same incident. We rarely see or experience anything without filtering it through our own persuasions or preconceived notions.

As a former children's pastor, I relied heavily on the Lord to continually give me unique ways and techniques to hear and see things to make the gospel come alive to my target audience. I have shared some of those techniques with you earlier in this book; here is another example. Many times while trying to make a point, God would break down words for me in a way a child could understand them. In the case of the word *perception,* that breakdown comes out to be *personal reception*—meaning how I personally receive it.

This is easily illustrated in the old story about two shoe salesmen who discover a remote island, fully inhabited with a native people who wear no shoes. One salesman wires back to his home office, "Forget it. Although there are many inhabitants here on the island, nobody wears shoes." The other salesman wires home and says, "Send me shoes of every size, color, and style. It's a completely open market, for nobody here wears shoes yet!"

Another example is the short poem that reads, "Two men looked through prison bars: one sees mud; the other sees stars." Perception is personal reception—how I take a thing in, how I process it!

This chapter's story is a combination of two events concerning the same group of people with a slight twist. These people hear of the same events twice, but are told the story by different witnesses to the events, which brings about two very different "perceptions" and then leads to two very different reactions. Let's read the Scripture texts now, and you'll see what I mean.

> So they arrived at the other side of the lake, in the region of the Gerasenes. When Jesus climbed out of the boat, a man possessed by an evil spirit came out from a cemetery to meet him. This man lived among the burial caves and could no longer be restrained, even with a chain. Whenever he was put into chains and shackles— as he often was—he snapped the chains from his wrists and smashed the shackles. No one was strong enough to subdue him. Day and night he wandered among the burial caves and in the hills, howling and cutting himself with sharp stones.
>
> When Jesus was still some distance away, the man saw him, ran to meet him, and bowed low before him. With a shriek, he screamed, "Why are you interfering with me, Jesus, Son of the Most High God? In the name of God, I beg you, don't torture me!" For Jesus had already said to the spirit, "Come out of the man, you evil spirit." Then Jesus demanded, "What is your name?" And he replied, "My name is Legion, because there are many of us inside this man." Then the evil spirits begged him again and

70

again not to send them to some distant place. There happened to be a large herd of pigs feeding on the hillside nearby. "Send us into those pigs," the spirits begged. "Let us enter them." So Jesus gave them permission. The evil spirits came out of the man and entered the pigs, and the entire herd of about 2,000 pigs plunged down the steep hillside into the lake and drowned in the water.

The herdsmen fled to the nearby town and the surrounding countryside, spreading the news as they ran. People rushed out to see what had happened. A crowd soon gathered around Jesus, and they saw the man who had been possessed by the legion of demons. He was sitting there fully clothed and perfectly sane, and they were all afraid. Then those who had seen what happened told the others about the demon-possessed man and the pigs. And the crowd began pleading with Jesus to go away and leave them alone.

As Jesus was getting into the boat, the man who had been demon possessed begged to go with him. But Jesus said, "No, go home to your family, and tell them everything the Lord has done for you and how merciful he has been." So the man started off to visit the Ten Towns of that region and began to proclaim the great things Jesus had done for him; and everyone was amazed at what he told them (Mark 5:1-20 NLT).

A short time later:

After they had crossed the lake, they landed at Gennesaret. They brought the boat to shore and climbed out. The people recognized Jesus at once, and they ran throughout the whole area, carrying sick people on mats to wherever they heard he was. Wherever he went—in villages, cities, or the countryside—they brought the sick out to the marketplaces. They begged him to let the sick touch at least the fringe of his robe, and all who touched him were healed. (Mark 6:53-56 NLT).

The first portion of our Scripture reveals the perception of the people the first time they encountered Jesus. The people asked Jesus to leave because they did not understand yet who He was. All they knew was that He was more powerful than the demons that had possessed the man in the cemetery, because He commanded the demons to leave the man and they had obeyed Him.

Remember how these people could not control the man? They tried several times, even chaining him up, and he had just broken off the restraints. They were afraid of the man and wanted nothing to do with him. Now here he was, sitting calmly at the feet of Jesus.

Mark 1 records a similar incident, but also lets us in on why the Gadarenes may have first reacted in fear and asked Jesus to leave their country. Jesus had confronted an unclean spirit in a man at the synagogue of Capernaum:

> Now there was a man in their synagogue with an unclean spirit. And he cried out, saying, "Let us alone! What have we to do with You, Jesus of Nazareth? Did You come to destroy us? I know who You are—the Holy One of God!" But Jesus rebuked him, saying, "Be quiet, and come out of him!" And when the unclean spirit had convulsed him and cried out with a loud voice, he came out of him. Then they were all amazed, so that they questioned among themselves, saying, "What is this? *What new doctrine is this?* For with authority He commands even the unclean spirits, and they obey Him." And immediately His fame spread throughout all the region around Galilee (Mark 1:23-28).

Jesus stood up to and took authority over the unclean spirit. The people supposed this was some new doctrine because Jesus did not speak as one mimicking something seen or taught, but as someone having true authority.

So here is Jesus with the madman of Gadara, sitting clothed and in his right mind, and the people show up terrified and beg Him to leave their country. They recognized He was more powerful and had authority over the unclean spirits, but they did not recognize Him yet as the Son of God.

Let's take a reality check here for a moment. The people did not recognize Jesus yet as the Son of God, but that did not make it any less a reality or the truth. The demons certainly knew who Jesus was; they were definitely afraid of Him, and they knew the power He possessed over them. Just hold that thought for a bit, and let's continue.

While Jesus is getting back in the boat to leave as the people have requested, the man once known as Legion begs Jesus to let him go with Him. Jesus says to him, "All is well; you'll be okay now. Go home to your family and tell them all that the Lord has done for you and how good He has been to you."

Jesus shows the importance of family when He says to the man, "No, friend, you don't need to come with Me. You need to go home to those who thought you were gone forever and rejoice at how good the Lord has been to you!" I am certain he did so, but his thankfulness spilled out into the streets of the surrounding towns. Come on! Jump into the pages of your Bible with me again. Imagine this man—now free, who most people had probably heard about only as the crazy man in the tombs—telling them, "I am he who was bound, but now I'm free."

Think of the passion and excitement he must have generated by telling them, "You called me Legion, for there were many devils in me. But Jesus has set me free, and He, my friends, is the Lord, the Holy One of Israel, the promised Messiah, the Son of God." So here we see the second telling of the same event that occurred that day on the shores of their country.

First we have the pig herders, probably both fearful and angry over losing their stock, running into town telling their version of what took place, which in turn brings the people out to see for themselves what is going on. They have mixed their hearing of the events with fear, and as it is recorded, they were terrified and begged Jesus to leave their country.

Now we have the man who actually experienced the events telling everyone what took place. Now they are not afraid, but amazed, and this causes them to begin to consider if Jesus could do the same for them and their families. Yes, they mixed their hearing now with faith!

How else can you explain what happens when Jesus returns to that region, as recorded in Mark 6:54? Read it again: "As soon as they got out of the boat, the people recognized Jesus." He is the same Jesus who was there in their country earlier, but now their perception of who He is has changed dramatically. Because of this change, they not only want Him to be there, but they are also counting on Him to do for all of them what he did for the man they once called Legion.

Our personal reception of Jesus will also determine what effect He has on our lives today, just as it did with the Gadarenes. Once they heard the message of Jesus—as spoken by the man now free—and mixed that message with faith, they saw Jesus not as someone to fear but as the Messiah, the Son of God, and they welcomed Him completely.

So what's your perception of Jesus and who is He to you? I can't help but think of the tenderness of the moment as Jesus is getting into the boat. This man wanted to go with Him; how full of compassion Jesus had to have been. The man was probably scared that if Jesus left him, the demons would return. And Jesus was quite aware of the man's thoughts and fears.

Listen again with me from the side of the boat as Jesus assures him that it's okay: "All is well; you'll be okay now. Go home to your family and tell them all that the Lord has done for you and how good He has been to you." As the man says, "But Lord…" Jesus might have continued, "No friend. You don't need to come with Me; you need to go home to those who thought you were gone forever and rejoice at how good the Lord has been to you."

Can you mix what you have heard today with faith? Can you personally receive all that Jesus wants to be in your life today? He wants to be the same for you today as He was for the man known as Legion. Hebrews 13:8 is your promise of that: "Jesus Christ *is* the same yesterday, today, and forever" (NLT).

If you have yet to receive Jesus as your personal Lord and Savior, could this be that day? If so, let's pray the prayer of salvation together found in chapter 20. If you already are a Christian, consider the following incident in a new light:

> So He came to Nazareth, where He had been brought up. And as His custom was, He went into the synagogue on the Sabbath day, and stood up to read. And He was handed the book of the prophet Isaiah. And when He had opened the book, He found the place where it was written:

> "The Spirit of the Lord is upon Me, because He has anointed Me to preach the gospel to the poor; He has sent Me to heal the brokenhearted, to proclaim liberty to the captives and recovery of sight to the blind, to set at liberty those who are oppressed; to proclaim the acceptable year of the Lord."

> Then He closed the book, and gave it back to the attendant and sat down. And the eyes of all who were in the synagogue were fixed on Him. And He began to say to them, "Today this Scripture is fulfilled in your hearing" (Luke 4:16-21)

What did you hear today? Can you believe beyond what you first perceived was possible? Can you mix your faith with the truths of this chapter and trust God with more than you did before? Whatever situations you may be facing right now, you're not facing them alone. So whatever you need to believe God for, just remember this: "The things which are impossible with men are possible with God" (Luke 18:27).

Faith Declaration: I believe and therefore I speak. Jesus is the Son of God and all things are possible to the one who believes. I believe my God shall supply all my needs according to His riches in glory. Regardless of my need—spiritual, physical, financial, or any other thing—today the Scriptures are fulfilled in my hearing as well.

Section II Review Page: Hearing

As you may now understand, hearing from God is not limited to only having an "experience" at church or somewhere else that you would expect God to be. The Spirit of the Lord is with us wherever we are, and just as you wouldn't expect your best friend or spouse to only talk to you when they are in a certain place, you should now understand that isn't the case with God either.

It's very important to remember that God will never speak to us beyond what He already has established through His written Word, the Bible, which means that when you believe you have heard from the Lord, it must be able to be proven by Scripture. Oh sure, we will hear things from God that will be new to us, as was the case when we received the word from our friend, Mary, about our daughter, Emily. But First Corinthians 12:7-11 confirmed God would speak to us that way, and wisdom gained through experience taught us how to accept what we had heard and how to act on it.

God will never violate His own Word and tell us some "new" thing that only we have discovered. God is a God of order. The purpose of Section II was to help you see and recognize the simplicity of hearing from the Lord.

As you read, most of the time what I heard came as a simple impression. It seemed as if it was just a thought that moved me, and that's because it was. It's what is known as an inward witness, an impression that you will learn to recognize as similar to just a thought, but with a little bit more urgency, so to speak. I have heard it described as "just something I knew I needed to pay attention to."

That was also the case in Chapter 8: "The Two-dollar Chicken Pot Pie." Lisa and I both had an inward witness that made us take notice of the lady in the story. We both heard the still, small voice of our own spirit cause us to refuse to settle for "it's the thought that counts." And I definitely heard the more authoritative voice of the Holy Spirit speak to me when He said, "Give her twenty dollars."

Hearing is easy. Learning to recognize the difference between our own thoughts and the Lord comes with practice, but it must be a process we are willing to go through as we continue moving forward in our relationship with the Lord.

It's kind of like me calling you on the phone. The first few times I probably would have to say, "Hey, this is Bobby Coleman," as I announced myself and then continued into our conversation. Eventually, though, you would begin to recognize my voice, because I still have a bit of a Southern drawl from growing up in Georgia, and there would be no need for an introduction before we started our conversation.

It's the same with the Lord. His gifts are perfect and He is perfect, but we are being perfected. For this reason, we must practice and learn through experience how to recognize and function in the things of the Spirit. Simply put, I just wanted to illustrate that God wants to converse with all His children, not just a chosen few as tradition or some denominations may teach.

Don't be afraid; God knows we will misstep. Remember—direction, not perfection. The key is that practice will certainly make us much better as we step out in faith. Just don't quit or refuse to continue moving forward. God has much more for us as we will "See" in Section III. Yes, Section III focuses on seeing the goodness of God and seeing things from God's perspective, so let's get to it and see what it's all about.

Section III: Seeing

Chapter 11: We're the Dirt Children, Grandma

*The blessing of the Lord makes one rich, and He adds no
sorrow with it.
—Proverbs 10:22*

It was 1996, and I had just reached another milestone in my
career—a third week of paid vacation. So after dividing my time
up for birthdays and some holidays, we found we still had enough
vacation time to make the big trip to Florida. My family was excited,
and so we planned, anticipated, and finally hit the road.

Marla and Aaron were thirteen and ten, respectively, at the time and
were assigned the back bench seat of our minivan. Timothy and Emily
were five and three and were in the middle row so Lisa could get to them
and keep them occupied. And so, with 1,300 miles of driving ahead, we
set out for Grandma's house.

I only remember now how crazy it was because we have our old
family videos to prove it. But after two days of driving with multiple
stops for fast food, gas, and bathroom stops, we pulled into the driveway
with loud screams of excitement and relief that we were finally there!

My folks' RV was set up just across the street from my Grandma
Bussell's vacation home. The RV park had a big community pool and
plenty of Florida sunshine. That alone would have been enough for me,
but the kids knew we were also only ten miles from our promised theme
park destination!

I was looking forward to just relaxing, grilling out, playing
horseshoes, and taking walks to get ice cream each night, but my kids
had only one agenda: When are we going to see our favorite characters

and go on the rides? It was our first time to this particular theme park so it was a big deal to the kids and to the rest of us as well. After some deliberations with my folks, we set a date, and with that much of our agenda now in order, we could settle in and "just be on vacation."

Marla and Aaron had come of age enough to see a familiar pattern whenever they were with Grandma and Grandpa Jim. Due to the distance between us and the limited amount of time we had to spend together, each year produced some predictable behaviors when we were together. My mom would readily admit it was an attempt to squeeze a year's worth of blessings for her grandbabies into the four or five days we got to spend together. It was a whirlwind of spending on the kids—clothes, toys, dinners, ice cream, you name it. As I soon found out, she had every intention of keeping this unspoken tradition going. We had just finished dinner one evening, and I was scraping the grill clean. My stepdad Jim was goofing around at the picnic table with Tim and Emily when my mom announced, "I think we should go shopping tomorrow."

Before I could say anything, our two older kids Marla and Aaron screamed out, "Yeah, all right, Grandma. Where are we going?" This in and of itself was no big deal; it's what they said next that really caught me off guard. My mom explained that to make things easier on herself she wanted to take the kids in shifts. First she would go alone with Marla and Aaron, and then afterwards, my mom, Lisa, Tim, and Emily would go on another day later in the week.

As she laid out this plan, our two older kids said to my mom, "You don't need to take Tim and Emily, Grandma; they have enough. We're the dirt children, and they're the golden children."

I was shocked and looked at the two of them and said, "What the heck does that mean?"

My dad burst out laughing, and my mom grabbed hold of Marla and said, "I know, honey. That's why Grandma is here." But I wasn't laughing; I was trying to decide if I was offended. I knew they were only thirteen and ten, but that sounded a lot like some kind of indictment on how Lisa and I treated our four kids.

I didn't say anything more at the time because my folks made light of it and smoothed it over pretty quickly. Quite frankly, I didn't know if anybody else took it quite as literally as I had. I learned long ago that even in criticism or jest there usually is some element of truth, and even though I believed that what my kids had just blurted out was way off-base and inaccurate, I had to wonder what they thought they were experiencing to make them say such a thing.

I admit there definitely were some distinctions between our kids. Marla and Aaron were close in age and so were Tim and Emily, and the five years that separated the two groups sometimes seemed like a much larger gap. I also admit that when Marla and Aaron were five and three, we were not nearly as prosperous as we had become by the time Tim and Emily were five and three.

So certainly the types and brands of clothing and shoes that Tim and Emily were wearing were of a much higher quality than we could afford when Marla and Aaron were that age. And we could afford for Tim and Emily to do things at that age that the older kids couldn't do at the same age. Because of this comparison, they were blind to what they were presently experiencing and able to do.

There were probably other contributing factors that Marla and Aaron based their opinion on as well, but without an adult's objective ability to reason, they could only go on what they could see and understand at the time.

The comparisons and the jealousies and insecurities that they so easily and readily seemed to invoke are age-old reactions that have come into play throughout human history. As a matter of fact, the very first recorded murder in the Bible was due to this very thing.

> Now Adam had sexual relations with his wife, Eve, and she became pregnant. When she gave birth to Cain, she said, "With the Lord's help, I have produced a man!" Later she gave birth to his brother and named him Abel. When they grew up, Abel became a shepherd, while Cain cultivated the ground. When it was time for the harvest, Cain presented some of his crops as a gift to the Lord.

Abel also brought a gift—the best of the firstborn lambs
from his flock. The Lord accepted Abel and his gift, but
he did not accept Cain and his gift. This made Cain very
angry, and he looked dejected.

"Why are you so angry?" the Lord asked Cain. "Why
do you look so dejected? You will be accepted if you do
what is right. But if you refuse to do what is right, then
watch out! Sin is crouching at the door, eager to control
you. But you must subdue it and be its master."

One day Cain suggested to his brother, "Let's go out into
the fields." And while they were in the field, Cain attacked
his brother, Abel, and killed him (Genesis 4:1-8 NLT).

When you are able to study this portion of Scripture in its original
language and understand the intent of certain words here, it makes
more sense than it does when you only read it at face value. I'm no
theologian, but I will try my best to do it simple justice for the sake of
our conversation. Basically, Cain and Abel brought their offerings to
God. Both brought from the bounty of their harvests; however, Abel
brought a very specific portion of his harvest, both the best and the first
portion of all he had reaped. Cain's offering implies that it was not from
the first portion of his harvest and further implies that it wasn't from
among his best either.

Without getting too deep here, further study suggests they both knew
what was expected, for God specifically spoke to Cain in verse 6 and
asked him why he looked so dejected, reminding him that he too could
have done what was right. God already had demonstrated during the re-
creation of the earth with Adam and Eve that like would beget like, and
that everything would produce after its own kind. So God's requirement
for them to bring their best and first was so He, too, could return to them
His best and first.

The first recorded sacrifice in Scripture would set the standard; Cain
and Abel's sacrifice would usher in God's returned sacrifice—His only
begotten son! Jesus was, and is, God's best and first. This is why God
could not accept anything less than Cain's best, and God warned Cain

that sin was crouching at the door of his heart, readily looking to control him if he refused to do what was right.

Comparison and jealousy can be traced back even to before the history of mankind, when Lucifer first compared himself to God and said, "I will exalt my throne above the stars of God…I will be like the Most High" (Isaiah 14:13-14).

So we can see where the dissatisfaction of comparison finds its roots and why it can have such an emotional drain on us and cause such deep resentment in us. It's been so from the beginning. I am sure we are not that sadistic or dark in our intent, but the story of my children illustrates how most of us get caught up in comparison and feel like we are missing out on our fair share. Whatever that is!

This is rooted in the work of Satan, and as adults we can see how this drives us and pushes us to be discontented with what we have so that we will push ourselves and overextend ourselves into the bondage of debt or a perpetual state of discontentedness which cannot be satisfied. What my older children were voicing was exactly this. They somehow felt that they had missed out on their fair share. Until I truly began to understand the message of grace and how God's original and still-prevailing intent is to bless those who call Him Father with abundance in this life, I regularly suffered from jealousy and insecurity.

My overwhelming belief was based on the misguided notion that blessing and favor were earned, and that placed me in competition with everyone around me for the blessings and favor of God. Seeing someone else being blessed somehow then proved that they had outperformed me or had been better than me, and they were sucking up my fair share.

One of the enduring traits that I have learned is how a person's actions expose their thoughts or intentions far more accurately than their words. In the case of jealousy, it exposes the error of our thoughts concerning the blessings of God in that we somehow believe God has a blessing quota and only has so much to go around. If we believe this, then it's possible that we believe that anyone who is being blessed or walking in the favor of God is potentially taking away from our own opportunities, or the amount to which we too can experience the blessings of the Lord.

Consider the Squirrel

This is why I took the time to reveal where the origins of jealousy were formed during the rebellion of Lucifer. If we subconsciously believe this—and I know from experience that many folks do, to some degree or another—then the blessings of the Lord experienced by others can actually form an underlying resentment toward God. When this happens, we are more susceptible to believing He is choosing a favorite, which is exactly what Cain had determined and is exactly what caused his demise.

This is also what my older children were thinking, and this was causing resentment in them as well. God is the God of more than enough. Whatever we need, God has it in abundance. Jesus himself said: "The thief does not come except to steal, and to kill, and to destroy. I have come that they may have life, and that they may have it more abundantly" (John 10:10).

We can expect to live a full and abundant life here on earth when we walk according to God's will and in fellowship with Him. We can and should rejoice with those who are being blessed, because God has more than enough to go around and my blessings are not dependent on anyone or anything other than God's grace and love for me. God has predetermined to bless us, and we can have full confidence that what He does for me and what He does for you is to lift us to a higher life, and our blessings certainly are not keeping either of us from having our full portion.

My granddaddy used to say, "Not only is the grass not greener on the other side, boy, but you can't see all the poop in it neither!" That might not be too scriptural, but I'm sure you get the point.

Faith Dedication: I rejoice when others are blessed and know that because God has determined it to be so, I declare I am blessed. I am empowered to prosper in all things—in my relationships, in my vocation, in my finances, in my health and wellbeing, and in life—because Jesus Himself said I would have life and have it more abundantly!

Chapter 12: The Kingdom of God Is Like…

But how can they call on him to save them unless they believe in him? And how can they believe in him if they have never heard about him? And how can they hear about him unless someone tells them? And how will anyone go and tell them without being sent? That is why the Scriptures say, "How beautiful are the feet of messengers who bring good news!
—Romans 10:14-15 NLT

Where we live in upstate New York, summers are filled with a series of fundraising events for local volunteer fire departments called the fireman's field days. Each community that has a volunteer department usually counts on these small fairs to raise a large portion of their annual operating budgets. Some towns even have parades, softball tournaments, and nightly fireworks displays to help bring in the large crowds necessary to fulfill the fire departments' budget needs. Now for people like my wife Lisa and I, this is where you want to be if you want to talk to people about the Lord.

As a disclaimer, let me say I too have had people approach me totally off-base in their zeal concerning how they spoke to me about God or faith issues. As a children's pastor, I certainly know the value of family time and rarely ever approached folks who are out with their kids. Our strategy focuses more on the traffic flow between the beer tents and the bathrooms.

I'm not kidding. Lisa and I literally held thousands of conversations over the years with people who were standing in line for a coveted portable toilet; we never really focused exclusively on getting people "saved" *per se*, but more on planting faith seeds. Jesus said:

> The Kingdom of God is like a farmer who scatters seed on the ground. Night and day, while he's asleep or awake, the seed sprouts and grows, but he does not understand how it happens. The earth produces the crops on its own. First a leaf blade pushes through, then the heads of wheat are formed, and finally the grain ripens. And as soon as the grain is ready, the farmer comes and harvests it with a sickle, for the harvest time has come (Mark 4:26-29 NLT).

Sometimes you have to introduce people to the understanding that God is a good God and He is interested in their wellbeing long before they will come to a place of wanting to make a commitment to Him or wanting to change the direction of their lives. Planting a seed of hope or the possibility that they still can take charge of their own lives with God's help and head in a new direction is very powerful and quite liberating.

I haven't run into too many folks to whom that the message of hope wasn't appealing. That's not to say I've never been rejected when sharing the good news of the gospel; of course I have. But valuing people's outlooks—where they presently are—is the beginning of validating where they could get to.

People are people. We all face the same fears of acceptance, success and failure, happiness and fulfillment, the pursuit of love, and so on. Further still, many of us have faced some very traumatic situations along life's way, and sometimes these things have hardened people to any number of understandable attitudes.

The worst thing that anyone could do to someone they just met is to tell them they are wrong for feeling the way they feel or responding to life however they have chosen to do so. My own childhood was seriously screwed up, and even now at fifty-plus years old I have to deliberately choose to overcome thoughts and attitudes that attempt to rise up at times.

To this day it is hard work for me to form relationships beyond surface levels. Oh, I can do it, but it takes a deliberate approach on my part, and I am sure you have issues of your own that are just as hard for you. So why would I, if I'm not even much of a people person, take the time to go and talk to strangers in public forums about the love of God? Because He loves me and rescued me, even from myself, when my life was a mess and my own foolish choices were making bad situations worse—that's why!

When Jesus began His public ministry, crowds flocked to Him because His message quite often focused on the contrast between what they had experienced in life and what they could have now. That's the approach that Lisa and I have employed for nearly thirty years when we are out among people sharing the gospel. I remember asking a guy once while standing in line for a portable toilet, "What's the good news?"

His response was: "No good news here, dude. Just drinking my troubles away."

So I asked him, "How's that working out for ya?"

He continued, "I ain't thinking about them right now. I ain't feeling nothing except that I got to go pee."

He told me a lot in thirty seconds. He had issues that he wanted to change and was trying the best way he knew to do so. Immediately challenging him or, worse yet, telling him that was the wrong way to fix them would have slammed the door shut to any further conversation.

Following the approach of Jesus and offering the contrast kept the door open as we continued talking. "I hear ya, man. Peace can be hard to find. I'm sure glad I did." Then I walked into my portable toilet. Did you really have any doubt he would be standing there when I came out? People are selfish by nature, and we always seem to want what others have, especially if we think it's better than what we've presently got.

I told him how I found my peace with God, and in spite of all the issues I was facing at the time, God gave me hope and the courage to face them instead of run away from them. The contrast was there, the seeds of change sown, and the focus of hope was squarely placed on having a relationship with Christ. We talked a little more, shook hands, and went our own ways. My contentment that I had accomplished my intended purpose was based on Isaiah:

> The rain and snow come down from the heavens and stay on the ground to water the earth. They cause the grain to grow, producing seed for the farmer and bread for the hungry. It is the same with my word. I send it out, and it always produces fruit. It will accomplish all I want it to, and it will prosper everywhere I send it. You will live in joy and peace. The mountains and hills will burst into song, and the trees of the field will clap their hands! Where once there were thorns, cypress trees will grow. Where nettles grew, myrtles will sprout up. These events will bring great honor to the Lord's name; they will be an everlasting sign of his power and love (Isaiah 55:10-13 NLT).

Seeds have to be planted, then allowed to grow, and when fully ripened, harvested.

When the thirty-year anniversary of a famous 60's music festival was held in Rome, New York, in 1999 it created all kinds of reactions from the communities surrounding the former military base that was used to host the event. This included picketing at the entrance gates from several churches and religious organizations denouncing the event and the people who planned to attend.

Lisa and I were members of a local church in Rome at the time, and our church actually applied for a booth permit and was granted full access for the entire event. Lisa and I—along with several other volunteer members of our church and our pastor who actually served on a medical team the whole weekend—set up our booth and loaded the tables with our wares. We had two-sided maps that contained a layout of the former base and all the festival's stage locations on one side and a map on how to get to heaven on the other. We had promise pins that symbolized a pledge for sexual purity until marriage, and other literature and small trinkets to give away. We also gave away thousands of bottles of water that had our church information and the way of salvation written on them.

Bobby Coleman

Our big catch items were multicolored Mardi Gras beads. We gave away cases of them, and as people flocked to our tables we literally spoke with hundreds of people. I remember many of the conversations I had with people who were amazed and intrigued that in the middle of all that hedonism, we were there too—the unashamed, open-armed church.

Yeah, sure, it was a little rough at times, and it certainly was no place for the faint of heart, but because we cared and weren't freaked out by all that was going on around us, we had people break down in tears because they realized we were there for them. We prayed with people for many things you probably couldn't imagine. We even held a service on Sunday morning, and people sat right on the grass in front of our booth and listened respectfully and intently.

We prayed with pastor's kids who had rebelled, a rabbi's son who finally felt he was in a safe enough place to ask about Jesus, people who had felt they didn't fit in at church, and plenty of folks who had little or no knowledge of God.

Even in the middle of a festival about sex, drugs, and rock 'n roll, we had girls with boyfriends in tow who wanted the purity pins and asked if they could have a do-over. Sometimes it was hard to hold the tears back ourselves.

I specifically remember one half-dressed, tattooed, and pierced young man who asked me, "How come you're not out front picketing with everybody else?"

My response was immediate: "Because God told me to be in here so I could tell you how much He loves you just the way you are."

You think the gospel can't hold its own? I beg to differ. I saw grown men and women wearing their bandanas and leathers break down and cry in front of everybody because our team members weren't afraid to put our arms around them and just hold them as they wept. The good news is good news! Even still, we had plenty of naysayers telling us we shouldn't have been there. People copped the same attitude with Jesus though, so we felt we were in pretty good company.

> Then Jesus went out to the lakeshore again and taught the crowds that were coming to him. As he walked along, he

91

saw Levi son of Alphaeus sitting at his tax collector's booth. "Follow me and be my disciple," Jesus said to him. So Levi got up and followed him.

Later, Levi invited Jesus and his disciples to his home as dinner guests, along with many tax collectors and other disreputable sinners. (There were many people of this kind among Jesus' followers.) But when the teachers of religious law who were Pharisees saw him eating with tax collectors and other sinners, they asked his disciples, "Why does he eat with such scum?"

When Jesus heard this, he told them, "Healthy people don't need a doctor—sick people do. I have come to call not those who think they are righteous, but those who know they are sinners" (Mark 2:13-17 NLT).

The gospel message has never been about dividing people; the world we live in is really good at that, but the church—that's me and you by the way—the church has been assigned the ministry of reconciliation.

So we have stopped evaluating others from a human point of view. At one time we thought of Christ merely from a human point of view. How differently we know him now! This means that anyone who belongs to Christ has become a new person. The old life is gone; a new life has begun!

And all of this is a gift from God, who brought us back to himself through Christ. And God has given us this task of reconciling people to him. For God was in Christ, reconciling the world to himself, no longer counting people's sins against them. And he gave us this wonderful message of reconciliation. So we are Christ's ambassadors; God is making his appeal through us. We speak for Christ when we plead, "Come back to God!" For God made Christ, who never sinned, to be the offering for our sin, so that we could be made right with God through Christ (2 Corinthians 5:16-21 NLT).

So if you ever get the chance or feel bold enough to strike up a conversation with someone and that opens the door for you to share the love of God with them, remember how Jesus did it.

Jesus said, "How can I describe the Kingdom of God? What story should I use to illustrate it? It is like a mustard seed planted in the ground. It is the smallest of all seeds, but it becomes the largest of all garden plants; it grows long branches, and birds can make nests in its shade."

Jesus used many similar stories and illustrations to teach the people as much as they could understand. In fact, in his public ministry he never taught without using parables; but afterward, when he was alone with his disciples, he explained everything to them (Mark 4:30-34 NLT).

The smallest of all seeds eventually becomes the largest of all plants. Hmm!

Faith Declaration: I have been given the ministry of reconciliation, and I know that even the smallest seed sown for the kingdom of God will produce according to Isaiah 55. God's Word will prosper wherever it is sent.

Chapter 13: It's Only a Matter of Time!

A single day in your courts is better than a thousand anywhere else! I would rather be a gatekeeper in the house of my God than live the good life in the homes of the wicked.
—Psalm 84:10 NLT

But you must not forget this one thing, dear friends: A day is like a thousand years to the Lord, and a thousand years is like a day.
—2 Peter 3:8 NLT

I knew this routine all too well. This was probably my third or fourth visit to the principal's office this year. When I got there, he was waiting for me. No, not the principal—my son Aaron. As usual, we went in together.

Aaron is now a gunnery sergeant in the United States Marine Corps, and has two awesome boys of his own which is a universe away from where we were at that moment. At this moment in time, we are at the junior high school and about to visit with the principal; the two of us were just short of a first-name relationship.

I don't remember this particular visit's infraction, but I do remember an exchange between Aaron and Mr. F., as we will call him. It went something like this:

Aaron: "Mr. F, this is the longest year of my life. I just want this school year to be over."

Mr. F: "Aaron, I want this year to be over too, but I want to give you a little insight about it. This year time has

95

not passed any faster or any slower for me than for you, but you are thirteen years old while I am fifty-seven. So this year has been one-thirteenth of your entire life and it looms very long and large to you. This same year is only one-fifty-seventh of my lifetime, and in that perspective, it has been a very short amount of time and has passed too quickly."

He went on to share with Aaron about goals and the purposes for his future and how to stay out of trouble in his math class for the next six weeks, so he could move on to high school and the rest of his life's journey or something along those lines.

I've used that short exchange between the two of them many times in various ways over the years, but it wasn't until I was trying to recall significant events that I wanted to include in this book that I saw its eternal perspective as clearly as I do now.

Nothing seems to slow the passage of time like a season of struggle. I think by nature we are all somewhat impatient. Which is why I believe one of the nine fruits of the Spirit is patience or longsuffering as it is recorded in Galatians 5:22. Longsuffering, though, doesn't mean what it sounds like—suffering for a long time. It actually means waiting patiently with a good attitude.

I shared the story about my son's struggles in middle school because it so easily demonstrates what happens with many of us when we go through seasons of struggle. We tend to shift our focus from what is going on to how long it has been going on. *Struggle* means to fight, to strive, to try very hard—all of which could probably describe our attitudes and actions at times when we face difficult situations. When we couple those attitudes with impatience, it's easy to see from the outside the perfect storm that could be brewing on the inside.

"But the fruit of the Spirit is love, joy, peace, longsuffering, kindness, goodness, faithfulness, gentleness, and self-control" (Galatians 5:22-23). I chose to include the entire list here because these are not generally the attitudes, actions, or deeds that we usually display when we are struggling.

Bobby Coleman

I used to get down on myself and withdraw, and then I'd be miserable to be around as I tried to push my way through the difficulty. Oh, and did I mention that no one wanted to be around me at those times either? I called this scenario, coupled with impatience, "the perfect storm" brewing on the inside, and here's why: We really are what we think. I'm not talking about positive thinking or some psychological semantic wordplay; those things are best left to the high and lofty. I'm talking about us at our core, and that's this: We believe we are what we tell ourselves we are, and what we repeat about ourselves in our minds. Of course it's not really the truth unless what we are telling ourselves lines up with what God's Word says about us.

I've said several times in this book that we are a spirit who has a soul and lives in a body, and this is true. We have established it's the spirit of a man that is born again, and that God is a Spirit and must be worshiped in the spirit, so what exactly does our soul do and what part does it play in our redemption?

Our soul is our mind, our intellect, our emotions, the way we think, the way we act and process, which is exactly why the Bible speaks of our spirit and soul as two distinct and completely separate features within mankind, with different purposes and functions. Before we get back to "the perfect storm" of our struggles, trials, and temptations, let's examine Scripture to establish some thoughts we will want to consider later.

> Now may the God of peace Himself sanctify you completely; and may your whole spirit, soul, and body be preserved blameless at the coming of our Lord Jesus Christ (1 Thessalonians 5:23).

> For the word of God is living and powerful, and sharper than any two-edged sword, piercing even to the division of soul and spirit, and of joints and marrow, and is a discerner of the thoughts and intents of the heart (Hebrews 4:12).

> Beloved, I pray that you may prosper in all things and be in health, just as your soul prospers (3 John 2).

97

Consider the Squirrel

> I beseech you therefore, brethren, by the mercies of God, that you present your bodies a living sacrifice, holy, acceptable to God, which is your reasonable service. And do not be conformed to this world, but be transformed by the renewing of your mind, that you may prove what is that good and acceptable and perfect will of God (Romans 12:1-2).

These passages clearly establish several key points that can help us in our struggles. First, God is a God of peace, and His complete sanctification for us involves not just our spirit but also our soul and our body. Second, the Word of God, our Bibles, will help us discern what is going on in our soul. Third, what and the way we think will affect our success and health. Fourth, the apostle Paul pleads with us to use the Word of God to renew the way we think and act in order to prove what is that good and acceptable and perfect will of God.

I had some really crazy ideas about love and acceptance based on many different experiences of my childhood and into the first twenty-five years or so of my adulthood. I couldn't just accept the love of God as a free, no-strings-attached gift, because embedded deep within my soul—my mind, thoughts, and emotions—was the idea that love and acceptance had to be earned and that you had to be worth something to someone to be loved or accepted.

Then came a struggle I just couldn't get away from. My emotions and thoughts were at a heighted sensitivity, I was miserable and withdrawn, I was just trying to push my way through, I felt invisible to God, my self-worth was at an all-time low, and did I mention I was laid off and unemployed? All that I was thinking only magnified with the length of time that was passing—just like my son, Aaron, back in middle school. My focus was on how long this struggle continued; I wasn't interested in trying to discern anything, I just wanted this process to be over.

Time as we know it is a mechanism God created on behalf of humanity for humanity. Time, even by itself, is an agent of change. Just by virtue of the passage of time, nothing remains the same, so God's focus in our lives is more about the changes taking place within us, rather than the time it takes for them to occur.

When we go through times of struggle—a better description might be a time of transition as I am describing here—God's intention is to bring about a discovery of purpose. God is looking to have us discover some things about ourselves. Very often the first stage of transition is conflict followed by a period of discomfort. But if we stay with it and see it through, it brings about blessings and abundance.

Now back to the particular transition that I was facing. I had lost my desire to read my Bible and was in a perpetual state of sulking (conflict followed by discomfort). While this was going on, I also was being somewhat deceitful because I tried to keep my countenance up before everyone. Some people rightly call this "wearing a mask," and I did it for quite a while.

They say it takes more muscles to frown than smile, and that same principle is true about faking happiness and peace: It takes more effort to do that than it does to apply God's Word to the situation and eventually overcome the thing (the blessings and abundance).

God's Word is God's heart and His will for people. Even though there are times when we might not know how to apply it to our situation or circumstances, it does not negate what He wants to do in our lives.

I finally came to the conclusion that this thing wasn't just going to go away. The issues that developed from my long stint of being unemployed, and all the secondary struggles that came along for the ride, weren't just one more thing from which I would find my way out. This was only going to change with the help of God and most specifically from the strength, wisdom, and discernment He promises us will come as we study His written Word. Take the promises literally and get moving!

This is why I mentioned that *transition*, what I was going through, is about "discovery of purpose." My life was taking on a very different focus and purpose than it had encompassed in my past. It was very conflicting, definitely causing discomfort. The blessings only came because I refused to quit, even when I had no idea what I was doing. Read on and see how.

I have to be honest and transparent. My Bible felt like a brick when I first picked it back up, and after a few rounds of Scripture roulette, I finally just held it in my lap and sat quiet before God. My thoughts were all over the place, but I said nothing. *It isn't supposed to be this hard*, I thought. Sitting before God is supposed to be refreshing, a peaceful experience, and it did eventually become that as I stayed with it.

After I gave up the idea that I was going to find that one-knock Scripture to end this struggle and see all my issues solved, I just began to read and read and read some more, and His Word brought enlightenment. Selah. (Pause and take a deep breath.) I learned to resist the devil and to speak in line with what God said, then I began to have what I said (Mark 11:22).

The attitudes and deep-seated beliefs I had were challenged and found to be contrary to what God's Word actually promised us as His children in times of trouble. It took a while for the discernment that Hebrews 4:12 says will come through God's Word to begin to dismantle the beliefs I had held on to throughout my life to this point.

I had nothing to make myself "worth it." I was out of good works and my own efforts. It was just me and my Bible, and so I began speaking forth what it said over myself. I would say things like, "Father, what You did for David, I know You will do for me, for You make no distinction between one man and another."

I began to thank Him for not just *a* job but *the* job, that job that would be the perfect fit for my talents and abilities with no limits or stipulations on salary or any other conditions. When bills would come in, I would lift them up and say, "Father, it's my desire to pay this right now. You know what we have, but according to Your Word, all my needs are met through your riches in glory in Christ Jesus." During this time we never stopped tithing!

It was mechanical and very deliberate for quite some time, but it was also what I knew I was supposed to do. Then I would just thank Him because Philippians says, "Be anxious for nothing, but in everything by prayer and supplication, with thanksgiving, let your requests be made known to God; and the peace of God, which surpasses all understanding, will guard your hearts and minds through Christ Jesus" (Philippians 4:6-7 NJKV).

Romans 12:1-2, as we just read a little bit ago, instructs us to replace the way we would naturally think in a struggle with what God's Word says. As I began to override my natural tendencies to get down on myself and give up my hope that things would change and choose to believe what the Bible said instead, it became much easier to speak the promises out loud once again. My Grandma Bussell used to say, "Bobby, sometimes you just gotta preach yourself happy!" This is exactly why I have included a faith declaration at the end of each chapter.

David, in the Psalms, so perfectly penned that God restores the soul, and the way He does it is by us immersing ourselves in His Word. Read, read, and read some more; then confess what it says in the first person. He restores my soul, He is my shield, He is my provider, He is my healer, and He is my help in time of need—you get the picture.

So while you might be in some type of struggle at this moment, you can never get enough of the Word, so again, "I beseech you therefore, brethren, by the mercies of God, that you present your bodies a living sacrifice, holy, acceptable to God, which is your reasonable service. And do not be conformed to this world, but be transformed by the renewing of your mind, that you may prove what is that good and acceptable and perfect will of God" (Romans 12:1-2).

Faith Declaration: God restores my soul through His own words; I believe the promises of God. I believe and therefore I speak and make the following declaration: I can have what the Bible says I can have, I will be who it says I can be, and I will do what it says I can do. I will do it today and keep moving forward!

Chapter 14: "Aim for the Bat"

*And I am certain that God, who began the good work within
you, will continue his work until it is finally finished on the day
when Christ Jesus returns.*
—Philippians 1:6 NLT

Ah, the days of summer—sitting on the porch swing, slowly
rocking, half dozing, and just enjoying the moment. It's rare
for most of us these days to truly have nothing to do, nothing
pressing, and nothing being ignored so we can have a few minutes to
really just sit and, well, do nothing and be okay with that.

I was having one of those moments when my boys caught me "doing
nothing" and started on me, "Come on, Dad, play ball with us."

"Nah," I replied. "Not right now. I'm comfortable. Maybe later."

But they persisted: "Come on, Dad, you're not doing nothing."

Exactly, was my thought, but after some reluctance I agreed, and the
game was on.

Well, this is how it went down: I was pitching, Lisa was playing
catcher, Aaron was playing in the field, and Timmy, who was about five
years old at the time, was batting. Now, I wasn't just pitching, I was
doing my cartoon character three-times-around-the-world windup and
high-leg kick delivery. Timmy couldn't hit a thing.

Now I'm kind of a pretty competitive guy, but this was my son,
and that's why Lisa finally yelled out to the mound, "Come on, Bobby.
Throw him something he can hit!"

So I glared in from the mound and said, "All right batter. Where ya
want it?" Timmy took some practice swings, pounded on the plate a few

times and then the real game was on. "All right, batter. Here it comes—a meatball right down the middle. Let's see watcha got!"

At first, nothing changed. But slowly I got Timmy's timing down on his swing and then did something no one was aware of at first but me: I started aiming for his bat and—you guessed it—he walloped that oversized plastic ball. After we did this for a while, Timmy's confidence began to grow, and he even started tracking balls out of the strike zone and was still making contact.

We played for quite a long time that day, and Timmy got to where he was swinging for our neighbor's pool three houses down before we finally decided it was time to quit and go get ice cream. I don't know how much of an effect it had on Tim's future, but he ended up playing baseball all the way into high school and even on a state playoff team.

Years later in 2003, I had to make a very substantial decision that would possibly affect our family's financial future for years. Lisa and I knew we needed to hear from God for sure, and so we agreed that I needed to go up to the Adirondack Mountains and fast and pray for three days to focus on the leading of the Lord. I came home and confirmed what she had also heard, and we made the decision we needed to make.

Now fast-forward a few more years with me, We were facing some very unfamiliar ground and were asking ourselves, "Did we do the right thing?" My confidence and self-worth were shaken and very low; I was really down on myself and felt like I totally missed God, which also caused me to be angry with myself. This is one of Satan's greatest ploys—to get us to blame ourselves and then believe we can't ask God for help.

I was having my John-the-Baptist-in-prison moment like I described to you back in Chapter 6. You remember—the whole doubt and questioning thing. I had all kinds of questions, and doubt was pulling hard against my faith.

Yet God is faithful and is not moved by our confusion. He got past all the clutter in my mind and simply reminded me about playing ball that day in the yard with my family and said to me, "I aim for your bat, too." I was surprised and excited, but still flustered.

Bobby Coleman

I didn't immediately jump up and do cartwheels across the lawn. Actually, I kind of just kept up my sulking, pitiful ways for quite some time, but I couldn't get what God had said out of my mind. It took a while, but eventually even a hard-head like me couldn't deny the depth of what God was saying. I mean, think about it. I knew Tim wasn't going to be able to hit the ball that day unless I helped him, and God knows we can't do what we need to do without His help either.

Unbeknownst to Timothy that day, I took the onus for his ability to make contact with the ball onto myself and adjusted what I was doing to guarantee he would succeed. After I got over enough of my pity party that I could consider what God had said to me, I realized that is what He does with me, and with you, every day.

God took on Himself the responsibility to make a way for us to be reunited with Him, and He dealt with the sin that was keeping us apart from Him on His own by sending His own Son to fulfill all that was required to free us from sin's bondage. God reconciled us back to Himself without any effort on our part, and then said, "Only believe."

A visiting minister once taught a message at our church about grace that was very different from anything I had heard before that. I'm sure at times, and maybe even now, you have done what I have done, which was hear about God's grace and how wonderful it is and then try to figure out how to be good enough to get it.

That's a sadistic merry-go-round that God never intended any of us to get on or, worse yet, push around for the others who are on it. We can't earn what God has decided to freely give us. Grace was and is God's idea and cannot be improved upon by human efforts. It's already perfect, and it's already ours by God's choice and design!

Without God we would be doomed, and He already knew that when He sent Jesus to take on the legal and spiritual ramifications of sin, which included separation from Him, so we could come home. I know it's woven deeply into our fiber that we have to fend for ourselves, and God did wire us that way, but that's there to give us the tenacity to press on and not quit; it's not there to encourage us to go it alone. Remember, at the fall of man, everything got jilted away from its original intent.

That's what sin does: It perverts just enough to destroy or deceive or deteriorate. (It also separated us from God.)

My confidence that God did not intend for us to fend for ourselves or go it alone is based on God Himself, for even He is not alone. He is the triune God of all creation, the three-in-one God, and it was God Himself who said at the beginning of mankind's days on the earth, "It is not good that man should be alone; I will make him a helper comparable to him" (Genesis 2:18).

So by God's design, we have both natural and supernatural help in this life, which is why what God was saying to me finally sank in, and now hopefully it will bless you as well: "I aim for your bat every day." God has our back, and oh, and by the way, your front, and yep, both sides too. We just need to remember the great length and sacrifice God was willing to endure to properly and legally redeem us from the mess that we found ourselves in through Adam and Eve's choices. God is for us; He wants and expects, by His own abilities that work in us, that we will win and be the victors in this life.

Don't just breeze through the faith declaration at the bottom of this chapter today, but really meditate on it and repeat it aloud through the remainder of your day. Yes, hold fast to your confession of faith. One last thing—that "hold fast to your confession" in the Greek actually means "say the same thing," and it refers to saying the same thing about yourself that God says about us. Plant your feet and say the same thing about yourself as God says about you!

Faith Declaration: My confidence is in the Lord. I am fully persuaded that God, who has begun a good work in me, will stay at it and bring it to completion in my life every day until Jesus returns. My confidence is in God, and He who knows my limitations also knows how to bring me up higher and into victory in spite of them today and every day. Today I will live out of my position in Christ and whose I am, rather than any temporary condition or where I am.

Chapter 15: I Can See That

*Because he has set his love upon Me, therefore I will deliver
him; I will set him on high, because he has known My
name. He shall call upon Me, and I will answer him; I will be
with him in trouble; I will deliver him and honor him. With
long life I will satisfy him, and show him My salvation.
—Psalm 91:14-16*

I heard a story some time ago that really stirred a serious conviction in me about living my life on purpose and with a true sense of priority. I hope to do the story justice and that it will have the same impact on you as it did on me.

A certain gentleman was enjoying his usual Saturday morning routine, which included reading the paper and drinking his coffee while quietly sitting at his table and listening to talk radio while the rest of his family enjoyed sleeping in. On this particular morning, he reached over to turn up his radio as he heard two gentlemen having a conversation.

The one sounded quite a bit older and much more relaxed, the other—the actual host—seemed hurried and pressed. The older man was talking to the host about a thousand marbles and how what he had discovered had changed his life.

The two men obviously had talked before they went on the air, for the older man was sharing with his much younger host his sadness that this young family man had to be away from home so much for work. Although he probably was compensated well, he felt the pain of his host missing out on so much of his children's lives, and what a pity it was that he had to work sixty-plus hours a week just to make ends meet.

Without so much as a response from his host, the older man continued with this statement: "I want to share with you something that has helped me keep my focus in life, and to remain true to my priorities." And thus began the story of the thousand marbles.

The older man continued by telling the host that the average man lives about 75 years or so—some more, some less—but with this number in mind, he multiplied 75 times 52 (the number of weeks in a year) and came up with three 3,900, which is the approximate total number of Saturdays we will have in our lifetimes.

After some additional quick math, the older man figured he had already lived out about 2,800 of those Saturdays, and if he lived out his life according to the average, he only had about 1,100 Saturdays or so left to enjoy. He continued by telling the radio host, "So I went to the toy store and bought enough marbles to represent my remaining Saturdays and put them in a large, clear jar in my workshop. Every Saturday since then I have taken one out and have thrown it away."

He told the host, "I have found over the years that watching the marbles slowly disappear has helped me remain focused and really helped me keep my priorities straight." The young radio host, making only an occasional sound of agreement, listened intently as the old man shared one last thing with him before he signed off so he could take his wonderful, loving wife to breakfast.

"This morning," he said, "I took the very last marble out of the jar. If I make it till next Saturday, then I believe God has blessed me with a little extra time to spend with those I love. I sure hope you are able to spend more time with those you love, too." With that he bid his young host farewell and expressed the hope that he might someday see him again.

The radio was silent; the host was speechless. Finally he muttered, "I guess he gave us all a lot to think about today."

The man who had been sitting at the table had his day already planned with his own activities, but instead, after hearing this conversation, he raced up the stairs and woke up his wife with a kiss. "Come on, Love, get up. I'm taking you and the kids to breakfast," he proclaimed. "And then, after, we need to stop at a toy store."

The same day I started writing this chapter I was in the grocery store with my daughter, Emily, and we were talking about her future—the whole thing: her job, finishing college, marriage, having kids. That led her back to how we raised her.

She was talking about how she wanted to raise her own kids similar to how she was brought up, and the first thing she said was, "I want to be able to take them to breakfast on Saturday mornings; I love all that you did for us, Dad." She had no idea I had already begun work on this chapter earlier that same morning. I smiled and hugged her.

I am going to make myself very vulnerable here. The rest of her statement to me was, "I know things have been really hard lately, but they won't stay this way." She also recalled how she was so thankful that when she was young, Lisa was able to stay home and be there for them.

During the writing of most of this book, I have been unemployed. I was laid off, and although it has given me the time to write this book, things have not always been easy. I know that many folks who held high-paying or at least very rewarding jobs are also without work and have experienced the same struggle to make ends meet and to keep their families going like we have.

Emily's expressed thankfulness about her mom being able to stay home was because my wife presently works two jobs in order to help us get through this time. Gone, for right now, are the breakfasts— and trust me, we all miss that. I was brought up in the South, and sitting around the table talking and "cutting up" was just second nature to me.

We may have had to change or even give up some of the things we once could afford, and some of those choices were harder for us to make than I thought they would be, but they did not affect the areas that we chose from the beginning to hold precious. We have held onto our convictions that family is first. We pulled together, and please don't take that to mean we haven't struggled or had to make sacrifices or even to do humbling things at times; but with all we have had to sacrifice, we haven't sacrificed each other.

Many of our priorities and life purposes have not been regulated by our temporary financial situation. I can—and do, on a regular basis—tell my wife and our children with sincerity that I love them. We all regularly check on each other by phone, text, or small notes in the morning. And you can too.

Whatever your present circumstances might be, life as illustrated in the story of the marbles is too short to waste, so what has happened up to this point doesn't matter nearly as much as what you personally do from this point forward. All types of stupid circumstances, past hurts, childhood tragedies, and self-inflicted wounds by poor choices might have got you to where you are today. Quite possibly you feel stolen from, and it all might be justified, but no one can steal your future from you. It's true that those who don't create the future they want must endure the future they get. At some point we must make the determination that not one more minute of our lives will be focused on what is behind us, but on what lies ahead of us instead (2 Cor. 5:17 NLT).

I've heard it said that you can't grab hold of your future if your hands are still full of your past. I want to challenge you today to make some choices for your future, and then encourage you to reset your priorities and life purposes. It doesn't matter how long it takes you to figure it out; just determine to do it and don't give in until you are satisfied! The apostle Paul sums up this challenge with this exhortation: "So be careful how you live. Don't live like fools, but like those who are wise. Make the most of every opportunity in these evil days. Don't act thoughtlessly, but understand what the Lord wants you to do" (Ephesians 5:15-17 NLT).

To overcome and prevail against the struggles of life, we had to form some determinations in our hearts about what we would and wouldn't do and how we would respond when life happens. Shortly after, I went back into my career field and at a much higher pay rate. In between, I also kept busy and served more at my church.

My pastor had us do an exercise some time ago in which he asked us to set aside some quiet time and list ten or so items that he called "the governing principles of our lives." It was very helpful to me, and you can do this too. Without considering your present situation or struggles, you can make a list of governing principles that, going forward, will guide you through life and help direct your decision-making processes from this point forward.

This is your time to fill your jar with marbles and choose to live your remaining days with a bigger and more deliberate purpose. My own list is a little longer than ten, but I am choosing to include it here so you have an example of what I am asking you to do.

After you determine your own list of governing values as single-sentence statements, go back through and write a brief paragraph under each that defines what that value means to you.

1. I continually strengthen my relationship with God.

2. I successfully fulfill the call of God on my life.

3. I live my life morally pure.

4. I love and honor my wife above all others.

5. I am a loving and excellent father and grandfather to my family.

6. I honor God with my body by leading a healthy lifestyle.

7. I am financially responsible and productive with all I possess.

8. I live my life in a manner that inspires others to know God.

9. I am constantly acting to improve the lives of others.

10. I live an organized and focused life.

11. I finish what I start and accept responsibility for my actions.

12. I play often; it keeps me young at heart and creative.

13. I am prophetic and seek to operate in the gifts of the spirit.

14. I am evangelistic for I am not ashamed of the gospel of Jesus Christ.

15. I am grace oriented; I allow love to govern my actions and human relationships.

Some of these might be self-evident, but they all have a descriptive paragraph under each statement. I want you to know these are the values I consider when I make decisions of any importance in my life. They direct how I conduct myself on a daily basis. My governing values are all rooted in who I am in Christ—meaning the life I now live I live for the glory of God—and so my governing values are what I use as a quick reference to determine how well I am doing.

In conclusion, let me make one very important qualifying statement here about my list, and your list, of governing values that you have now determined to live by. Some of these values might be new directions, or what you have just determined to do, and some might not have been truths in your past.

I have several values on my list I had never really acknowledged to the degree I do now. I also have several that I must regretfully say were not always true or of great priority in my life. You may come across a similar situation when creating your own list. Remember, just as the older gentlemen with his marbles came to some realizations a little later in his own life, you and I will too.

Your list is the defining and redefining of what your life's focus, priorities, and purposes will be governed by as you go forward, because forward is the only direction worth pursuing. As in many of the conclusions that arise while reading this book, don't discount whatever emotions this exercise might bring up in your life, but choose to go beyond them. Don't get stuck!

Forgive and live. I can only pray you see the total value of choosing to let go of the past, good or bad, so you can set the values for your life that will govern your remaining days. Plan to do something this Saturday that will be your personal reminder that your life has a purpose and that you are passionately pursuing what that is.

Faith Declaration: Living my life with, and on, purpose will require the discovery of God's will for my life according to Proverbs 16:9: "A man's heart plans his way, but the Lord directs his steps." My life, no matter what it has held to this point, will not be defined by what it has been, but rather what I choose to make it become now—by God's direction.

Section III Review Page: Seeing

Jesus asked the crowds, "How can I describe the kingdom of God? What story should I use to illustrate it?" He understood beforehand that His listeners needed something tangible that they could see and recognize in order to relate to the truths He was about to teach them.

Section III has been my attempt at that very same thing, for as I said in the introduction of the book, Jesus used parables to more accurately explain the kingdom of God through relative, everyday circumstances and people, because the religious teachers of the day had confused the issues.

My attempt to do the same has been for the same reason. Today more than ever it seems people are truly confused about who God is and how He wants to relate to us. So how did I do? Each of the stories in Section III had a very definite purpose and theme, so to speak, that I believe the Lord wanted to help you "see."

1. God gave us His best when He sent Jesus to be the Lamb who takes away the sin of the world. His grace (undeserved favor) is a gift to each of us individually and should not be compared to another's blessing, for we have no idea what each of us need or in what season we need it. We can trust the Lord about that because the Lord does know what we need and when we need it.

2. God's kingdom principles work in my life similar to a seed sown in the ground; although it may begin as a small seed, it will grow and produce a harvest.

3. Seeing things from God's perspective can remove a lot of frustration, especially when it comes to the passage of time.

In every season of life, God will be right there with us, even when we don't understand.

4. Oh, how telling it was for me to see how orchestrated God is in His desire to have us succeed. We may not always hit a home run, but it sure is wonderful to know that He is aiming for our bat.

5. Living life on purpose and determining how we will do that empowers us to overcome unexpected obstacles and avoid some of life's pitfalls. This comes from predetermining what values we will live by.

Determining to move forward and hearing and seeing how God's kingdom and Spirit affect our everyday lives will certainly also have an effect on what and how we believe. Section IV focuses on just that, believing, and as was the case throughout the book, this next section has been designed to have you take some corresponding actions.

So forward we go.

Section IV: Believing

Chapter 16: A Field Left to Itself Goes to Weeds

Therefore we do not lose heart. Even though our outward man
is perishing, yet the inward man is being renewed day by day.
For our light affliction, which is but for a moment, is working
for us a far more exceeding and eternal weight of glory,
while we do not look at the things which are seen, but at the
things which are not seen. For the things which are seen are
temporary, but the things which are not seen are eternal.
—2 Corinthians 4:16-18

Before we relocated to Florida, we lived in a region of upstate New York known as the Mohawk Valley, which is just below the foothills of the Adirondack Mountains. From mid-July until about mid-October or so, it almost seems like the whole region turns into one giant farmer's market of roadside vegetable stands.

Over the years as a lineman for the phone company, I probably was up and down every highway and back road in the entire valley. I can remember many times driving along those roads, high up above most other vehicles in my line truck. It was easy, from that viewpoint, to notice many of the farms and especially how the corn grew. Sometimes when I was driving, I could look down the corn rows and they just seemed to flow like water. I'm not a farmer, but I noticed several interesting observations about those cornfields and growing corn over the years.

One of those observations is the folk saying, "Knee high by the Fourth of July." And every year, it really does seem to prove true that if the corn is at least knee high by then, everything is on schedule for a bountiful harvest. Once you see the blades breaking through the soil, you can't help but watch the progress of the corn and look forward to seeing the first fresh ears show up at your favorite roadside stand.

There's another observation that is probably missed by some, but was quite striking to me one spring morning when I noticed it. My line partner, Mike, and I were stringing a new telephone cable along a pole line just off the road. I was high up in my bucket, attaching the new cable to an existing cable run as Mike drove forward ever so slowly.

As you inch forward, pole after pole, pulling the cable into place, you have plenty of time to think and to look around and see what others at ground level can't see. I was looking out over a cornfield when we came up to another large field a farmer had decided to leave fallow for the year. Sometimes after many years of planting and harvesting, a farmer will leave a field undisturbed and unplanted for a year so it can rejuvenate and replenish its soil.

It's not an unusual sight, but this particular day I saw something in that field as I looked down on it that struck me as odd. In my spirit I heard, "A field left to itself goes to weeds." Let me first explain to you what I saw; later on, the Lord opened up my understanding to see what He meant.

From my vantage point, I could see the field had not been turned over or plowed earlier that spring. The fields on both sides of this one had neat, straight rows of freshly planted corn with new blades about six inches high, but this field still had last year's cut-off cornstalks in it with weeds growing faster than the corn in the fields on both sides of it.

As I saw the overgrown field and thought within myself, "A field left to itself goes to weeds," I realized that every year the farmer tilled that field, planted his corn, and then used all kinds of fertilizers and pesticides and weed killers to keep that field pristine and primed for growing his corn. But in only one winter and a few short weeks of spring, it had already returned to weeds.

I held on to what I heard that day and repeated it back to myself occasionally, whenever I'd see an overgrown field. Finally one day, out of the blue, I got the rest: This was the perfect picture of mankind. Letting a field lie fallow is a correct and common agricultural practice, but in the sense that it applies to the soul, it perfectly illustrates how quickly we can turn astray without deliberate maintenance of our thoughts and actions.

The Old Testament is filled with type and shadow illustrations and rituals to reinforce what God was preparing to do through the coming Messiah. Jesus' work on the cross on behalf of all humanity was the ultimate fulfillment of all those illustrations.

The field, in our illustration, is worked by the farmer. Plowing, planting, fertilizing, spraying pesticides and weed killers, and finally harvesting is a cycle that is repeated year after year. Yet the first year he breaks the cycle, the field immediately reverts. With the farmer's help, the field reaches its full potential to produce and reproduce, but left to itself it goes to weeds. Unfortunately, the earth came under a curse at the fall in the garden of Eden. Unless we are willing to constantly maintain our homes, possessions, relationships, and most importantly our faith, they too will begin to deteriorate and revert back to a less-developed state.

All that this world offers must be maintained in a constant cycle of renewal. Metal will rust, painted wood will peel, mortar will crumble, and relationships will fail. We are very much like the field in several ways; we too, left to ourselves even in the best of circumstances, cannot produce what is necessary or become good enough to reach heaven; mankind's fall was a spiritual issue that affected our natural circumstances.

It took God Himself to intervene and work our field, so to speak, and to do something in the spiritual realm that would reorder our natural realm. That something was sending His only Son. When God created people, He created us in His own image and gave us the ability to choose our own destiny; we are free moral agents with the ability to choose whichever path we want—very unlike the rest of God's creation.

Giving us the right to choose might seem like a huge mistake on God's part, considering the fall of Adam and Eve and all the mess that followed it, but it had to be that way if we were going to truly be created in God's image. Satan, who had already rebelled and been cast down out of heaven, believed that if he could deceive the man and woman in the garden and get them to disobey God as he had, he could forever doom all people to the same fate as his own.

Satan missed one vitally important fact though. Man, who could choose to disobey God of his own free will, could also choose to accept forgiveness and redemption and be restored to his rightful place in God's kingdom. This is what sets us apart from all the rest of creation. We are not a field left to ourselves!

When sin entered the world through Adam and Eve's choice to eat of the tree of the knowledge of good and evil, the Bible says their eyes were opened to see both good and evil and they now saw their own nakedness as shameful and hid themselves from the presence of God. They covered their nakedness with fig leaves, but God, who knows all things for all eternity, made them clothes by shedding the blood of an innocent animal and using its hide to cover their exposure to sin. He knew He had given them the right to choose, and unlike a fallen angel who had no recourse, humanity could still choose to follow God and receive forgiveness.

Thus, the shedding of blood and the sacrifices became a symbol of forgiveness, but this was only a temporary fix and a constant cycle of renewal which also kept them aware of their fallen condition. This was not a punishment from God, but a way of hope and a way to direct mankind to what would become a permanent forever fix—the shedding of the blood of Christ, a once-and-for-all, complete cleansing.

I am simplifying the plan of redemption here into a few short paragraphs; there is so much more to it, but what I want to get across to you is this: God doesn't need our futile attempts to reach Him by our own works and self-justifications. He reached out to us, covered our sin from the beginning, and made a way for us to have restored fellowship with Him because of His great love for us.

What is available to us today through the shed blood of Jesus and the cross is a permanent and complete redemption. A man is an eternal spirit who has a soul and lives in a body. Sin separated man's spirit from God the Father, rendering his spirit dead. Salvation is the quickening—or in simpler terms, the rebirth—of our spirits. Thus the term "born again."

Salvation restores us spiritually to God. After we are born again, we still live in our same old body. But God has a plan for that too:

> For we know that when this earthly tent we live in is taken down (that is, when we die and leave this earthly body), we will have a house in heaven, an eternal body made for us by God himself and not by human hands. We grow weary in our present bodies, and we long to put on our heavenly bodies like new clothing. For we will put on heavenly bodies; we will not be spirits without bodies. While we live in these earthly bodies, we groan and sigh, but it's not that we want to die and get rid of these bodies that clothe us. Rather, we want to put on our new bodies so that these dying bodies will be swallowed up by life (2 Corinthians 5:1-4 NLT).

We don't need to be like the farmer's field that must go through the same cycles year after year to maintain a certain level of presentation. The farmer is well aware that if at any time he stops this cycle of renewal, the field will revert.

With a born-again spirit and the promise of complete redemption, which includes a new body in heaven, our goal now is to cooperate with the leading of the Holy Spirit as a means of reaching our full potential in Christ, just as the field can only reach its full potential with the help of the farmer. God does not deal with us only at the level of our soul—the way we think, feel, or react. God deals with us according to our spirit and restores us spiritually, not mentally, to our proper standing with God. We can't just think we are okay with God; we have to accept doing things His way. He alone knew what it would take to restore mankind as we were in the beginning.

I know we all have our ideas at times about how God operates, but one thing is for sure—God created us in His own image to be like Him and to fellowship with Him. The parable of the sower spoken by Jesus actually says the Word of God is seed, and he who receives it into his heart and understands it is good ground and will indeed bear fruit (Matthew 13:23). We are the field that is the workmanship of the Lord if we choose to believe and cooperate with Him.

Consider the Squirrel

Thank God He did not leave us to fend for ourselves and then die. We are the redeemed and forgiven. If you have accepted the work of the cross and what the shed blood of Jesus has restored to us, rejoice and live. Live your life to its fullest; seek to know God's will for your life; and just as the field reaches its full potential for harvest with the farmer's help, reach yours now with God's help.

If you are not born again but believe now is the right time, pray this prayer of salvation:

> Dear God,
>
> I come to You in the name of Jesus. I believe in my heart that Jesus died on the cross for me—to break the power of sin and death over my life. I ask You to forgive me of my sins and to cleanse me from all unrighteousness. I confess with my mouth that Jesus is Lord and Savior of my life. Thank You for saving me. I accept this initial work of the Holy Spirit in my life and now believe that I am a child of God and You are my heavenly Father. In Jesus' name I pray. Amen.

Faith Declaration: I have been crucified with Christ; it is no longer I who live, but Christ lives in me; and the life which I now live in the flesh I live by faith in the Son of God, who loved me and gave Himself for me (Galatians 2:20 NJKV).

Chapter 17: What Does It Mean to be Born Again?

So we have stopped evaluating others from a human point of view. At one time we thought of Christ merely from a human point of view. How differently we know him now! This means that anyone who belongs to Christ has become a new person. The old life is gone; a new life has begun! And all of this is a gift from God, who brought us back to himself through Christ....
—2 Corinthians 5:16-18 NLT

As I was growing up in Michigan back in the early '70s, my dad began to develop the entrepreneurial spirit that eventually led to him owning several very successful businesses. But it all started with him being a part-time party host. He used to put on large-scale, reception-like events as one of his first business ventures. It was kind of like having a wedding reception without the wedding.

He would pick themes to generate excitement for each event, then sell tickets, hire a band, cater the food—you get the idea. New Year's Eve didn't need a theme and was always on the list, but I remember one summer event very specifically, because it was a Hawaiian luau. My dad did something else for that event that always made it stand out to me. He arranged for me to sing with the band. It was only one song, but I had to go practice my one song several times with the band before the big night.

I don't remember the name of the band or any of the members' names, but I do remember the keyboard player because I talked with him the most. He was blind, and I was very curious about how he could play that electric piano so well without seeing the keys. Sometimes as we were talking, I would forget he was blind and just talk to him about normal stuff. At other times, I would ask him questions specifically related to his inability to see.

He had been born blind and told me that he used his other senses to see. I think I was about eleven years old at the time, so I had to have him explain that to me because I had no idea what he meant. He had me take his hand and put it on my head and said, "You have short hair. I can feel it, and so that is how I see." He told me he used his memory to walk around in his house and not get lost, and eventually I began to catch on. Sometimes I would close my eyes and try some of the things he said.

The night of the luau, before everyone began to show up, I watched as the final preparations were being completed. I was on the stage and remember telling the keyboard player what was going on around us and telling him about this really cool water display right in the middle of the dance floor. It had a little bridge that spanned over fountains and had colored lights that rotated through the water spray. I just assumed he knew what I was talking about and figured that describing everything in great detail would help him "see it."

I remember this particular conversation because I had asked my friend if he could see the lights from the water show. They were very bright, so I wondered if he could see them. He said, "I can tell," as he pointed in the direction of the lights, "that it is brighter in that area over there than it is over here," and he pointed his finger away from the lights. I asked him if he could see the colors, and he said no—just brightness and darkness.

It's been nearly forty years since that night, and I've rarely thought of that luau except when I occasionally hear the song that I sang on oldies radio or in times like this when I have allowed the Lord to use different events in my life to open my understanding about His kingdom.

I'm not quite sure how to qualify this other than to say it seems to be the understood opinion of people much smarter than I that those who suffer from a disability generally have their other senses developed to a higher degree as a means of compensation. That did seem to be the case with my friend the keyboard player, way back then, as well as my friend, Matt, who is deaf. He has also confirmed that, at least in his case, he believes this to be true.

I bring this up for a really good reason and believe it could be very helpful in my attempt now to explain an often misunderstood central Bible truth—salvation—and most specifically, the term "born again."

First, let me set the standard I have used throughout the writing of this book as nothing other than the Bible. Certainly, the Bible must be held in higher regard than our traditions or denominational teachings. Several times to this point I've asked you to jump into your Bible and really use your own senses to see and experience what was going on. This is another one of those times. Ready? Jump!

> There was a man named Nicodemus, a Jewish religious leader who was a Pharisee. After dark one evening, he came to speak with Jesus. "Rabbi," he said, "we all know that God has sent you to teach us. Your miraculous signs are evidence that God is with you."
>
> Jesus replied, "I tell you the truth, unless you are born again, you cannot see the Kingdom of God."
>
> "What do you mean?" exclaimed Nicodemus. "How can an old man go back into his mother's womb and be born again?"
>
> Jesus replied, "I assure you, no one can enter the Kingdom of God without being born of water and the Spirit. Humans can reproduce only human life, but the Holy Spirit gives birth to spiritual life. So don't be surprised when I say, 'You must be born again'" (John 3:1-7 NLT).

Can you imagine how this had to affect Nicodemus? The struggle within him to understand had to be immense. All he could utter to this statement was, "What do you mean?" Jesus knew this would be hard for Nicodemus to grasp because his response began with, "I assure you."

It has been my endeavor throughout this book to take some of the more complex issues of Scripture and break them down into simpler, easier-to-understand examples from our everyday life experiences. This method of teaching has seemed to always have a positive effect on the folks I am sharing a conversation with—particularly for people who have no or very little Bible knowledge. Whatever your present state might be, I am thankful you have chosen to take up this book and discover who God is and the ways of His kingdom for yourself.

Nicodemus was drawn to the Lord, and as a respected religious teacher himself, he needed answers to the questions that burned in his heart. He acknowledged that Jesus was sent by God to teach them and even stated, "Your miraculous signs are evidence that God is with you."

The way Jesus replied to Nicodemus sets a distinction that is imperative for us to see. Nicodemus was basing his conclusions concerning the reality of the kingdom of God only on the natural evidence that he had seen and experienced. Jesus wanted to make it clear that seeing evidence that the kingdom existed versus actually seeing the kingdom were two different things, and that in order to actually see the kingdom of God, he was going to have to be born again.

This was based on the personal knowledge and understanding that Jesus had concerning the ways of the Spirit, for only He could fully explain the difference between human life and the spiritual life. What did He mean then when He said that people had to be born again of the Holy Spirit to enter the kingdom of God?

Back in the garden of Eden, God created Adam as a three-part being. First and foremost, Adam was an eternal spirit as God himself is a Spirit, and he was created in His likeness, had a soul, and lived in a body. In the garden, Adam existed in such a complete state of harmony within himself that there was no real distinction made concerning his makeup. The glory of God surrounded him, and it wasn't until Adam and Eve were deceived and separated from God by sin that they even realized they were naked.

Harmony was broken, and self-discord became mankind's new normal state. This was the result of death and spiritual separation from God. The Bible says Adam and Eve died the day they ate the fruit. "And the Lord God commanded the man, saying, 'Of every tree of the garden you may freely eat; but of the tree of the knowledge of good and evil you shall not eat, for *in the day that you eat of it you shall surely die*'" (Genesis 2:16-17).

128

Adam and Eve continued to live on the earth after this, so what did God mean "for *in the day* that you eat of it you shall surely die"? The word *death* here actually means *separation*, and most specifically separation from God. Adam remained a spiritual being who had a soul and continued to live in his body, but now he was spiritually dead and separated from God. Humans lost their harmony with God. In the beginning, they were created as spiritual beings whose souls were in complete unison to the will of their spirits, and their bodies followed the will of their souls in fellowship and love for God. But *in that day*, Adam and Eve's spirits were separated—dead to the things of God—or disabled if you will, meaning their spirits could no longer function as they were created to.

I say "disabled" because, even back then, people began to rely on their other senses to compensate for this loss and began to reason and allow their desires to overrule what they once knew as truth. This is also true with us today. We are spiritual beings, and we just can't function the way we were created to with separated, dead spirits. We also compensate for the condition of our spirits by elevating the functions of our souls and bodies—our thoughts and desires rule us. Our understanding and desire for a relationship with God have become distorted by how we think and feel; the only way to bring harmony back is by becoming born again.

Jesus came to the earth and lived His life as a sinless man, conceived by the Holy Spirit. His soul and body were created exactly as God had first created man, allowing Him to function as both the Son of God and the Son of Man. His purpose was to reconcile us back to God and to Himself by restoring the spiritual order that had been disrupted by Satan's deception of Adam and Eve. He did for us what we could not do for ourselves by His death and resurrection—Jesus restored our ability to be reunited spiritually with Father God.

> Once you were dead because of your disobedience and your many sins. You used to live in sin, just like the rest of the world, obeying the devil—the commander of the powers in the unseen world. He is the spirit at work in the hearts of those who refuse to obey God. All of us used to live that way, following the passionate desires

and inclinations of our sinful nature. By our very nature we were subject to God's anger, just like everyone else. But God is so rich in mercy, and he loved us so much, that even though we were dead because of our sins, he gave us life when he raised Christ from the dead. (It is only by God's grace that you have been saved!) For he raised us from the dead along with Christ and seated us with him in the heavenly realms because we are united with Christ Jesus. So God can point to us in all future ages as examples of the incredible wealth of his grace and kindness toward us, as shown in all he has done for us who are united with Christ Jesus. God saved you by his grace when you believed. And you can't take credit for this; it is a gift from God (Ephesians 2:1-8 NLT).

Paul wrote this to born-again believers in Ephesus to explain what happened to them at salvation—that in the heart and mind of God the Father they had been restored to their rightful position of fellowship with Him. Our task now, as it was with the Ephesians, is to make this restoration a truth in our everyday lives.

I know this might be somewhat hard to understand, so let's go back to my friend, the keyboard player in the band. He was born with eyes that just didn't see. He had all the equipment, so to speak, but his eyes didn't function as they had been created to do. My friend had evidence that sight was possible. He could distinguish between light and dark, but he had no actual sight. Again, his eyes were in place, but could not function correctly. Our spirits are in place too, but they can't function correctly either—until they are born again.

Matt can hear ever so slightly, but if he was completely deaf and unable to hear any type of sound at all, that certainly wouldn't mean that sound didn't exist. This is also true about the kingdom of God. Many people mistakenly believe that it doesn't exist based on their own experiences.

Sight exists, sound exists, and, my friend, so does the kingdom of God. The only way to truly experience it, see it, and enter into it is by following the words of Jesus:

I assure you, no one can enter the Kingdom of God without being born of water and the Spirit. Humans can reproduce only human life, but the Holy Spirit gives birth to spiritual life. So don't be surprised when I say, "You must be born again" (John 3:5-7 NLT).

The Holy Spirit gives birth to spiritual life; it's a supernatural work that doesn't require your understanding. Just as the fall did not change the human soul and body, neither does becoming born again. You will still think what you used to think and crave what you used to crave, but once your spirit is born again you can truly take the lead and change what you think, crave, and believe.

Spiritual harmony within you will be an ongoing work because, as I have said earlier, we learned to overcompensate and rely on our soul and body beyond their original intent. As a born-again child of God, all your problems will not magically disappear, but you will have fellowship with God and be able to ask for His guidance and favor to master life's problems and to change what you think according to God's Word.

My friend, if you have yet to ask Jesus Christ into your life, don't hesitate. If you believe in your heart that He died on the cross and was raised from the dead, then know also that His purpose for doing so was to bring you home. If you would like to pray a simple prayer with my help to ask Christ to come into your life, then pray out loud the prayer of salvation found on page 153, and then by faith proclaim, "I am born again."

Faith Declaration: I do believe even though I cannot see; I walk by faith and not by sight and base my salvation on the truths of the Bible only!

Chapter 18: Who's Your Daddy?

Then God said, "Let Us make man in Our image, according to
Our likeness; let them have dominion over the fish of the sea, over
the birds of the air, and over the cattle, over all the earth and over
every creeping thing that creeps on the earth." So God created
man in His own image; in the image of God He created him; male
and female He created them. Then God blessed them, and God
said to them, "Be fruitful and multiply; fill the earth and subdue
it; have dominion over the fish of the sea, over the birds of the air,
and over every living thing that moves on the earth."
—Genesis 1:26-28 NLT

Man, it was an awesome day for the first week of March in upstate New York. It was sunny and about 65 degrees, and I just had to take in a deep breath of fresh air and smile. I was in the drive-thru lane at my favorite coffee shop, and as I sat there waiting I was thinking about the message my pastor had shared just a few days before about the fatherhood of God. That's when God asked me, "So what do you think—did I create man to worship Me or to fellowship with Me?"

I immediately began thinking about the more prominent names of God—the King of Kings, the Lord of Glory, the soon-coming King, and so on. But then I answered, "Hmm, Father, You already had the angels to worship You; I think Your original intent was so we could fellowship together."

That's when He started to bring back to my remembrance our Scripture text above. I went through it in my mind as I was driving home with my coffee and considered—why did God say "in Our image and likeness"? Weren't they both the same thing?

Consider the Squirrel

As I began to study, I found that *image* refers to when one thing looks like something else, and *likeness* is more about something acting like another. So my understanding of what God was saying here was: "Let us create man to look like Us and act like Us." That, however, wasn't the answer to the question God posed to me in the drive thru—or was it?

A closer look at the context of our Scripture with this understanding in mind does reveal the answer, so let me set this up for us. Here we are, looking in on the beginning of humanity's existence on the earth. God has reworked the earth, its surface, and its atmosphere into a habitable place to sustain life, and then He says, "Let us make man to look like Us and act like Us." What God does and says to Adam and Eve immediately after they are created answers the question He asked me. He blessed them and gave them their first instructions.

Throughout Scripture, the word *blessed* is best interpreted as "empowered to prosper." That sounds like God, doesn't it? He certainly has all power and everything He does prospers. So creating mankind to look like Him and act like Him starts out with Adam and Eve looking like the image of God and then being empowered to act like Him. Got it?

What Father God says to them next is a list of how everything on the earth will be subject to their dominion and how they are to guard and keep the earth, right? I mean, God says rule over everything. At least, that is how most of us read and understand this passage, and that is and was God's original intent. However, the deceptive and treacherous act of Satan messed that all up for a while. But if this is all we gather— and it is what we almost always do—then we've missed one vitally important fact.

I want you to slow down and deliberately listen with your heart to what I am about to say. Immediately after God created Adam and Eve and empowered them to prosper, the *first* thing He commanded *before* "Rule the earth and everything in it" was "Have many children," or as the King James version says, "Be fruitful, and multiply."

Give me a little liberty here and imagine this conversation between God and the first humans with me: "Okay, I created you to look like Me, and I have empowered you to prosper, so here is how you act like Me and have the same attitudes as Me—have sons and daughters and rule the earth."

I am almost concerned you will miss this as I labor to simplify it. The very first attitude or attribute that God passed on to Adam was to be a Father, then a ruler—fellowship before worship. God's original intent was family! We were created to be what no other creation could be—God's own family.

Oh please, tell me you can see this. Take off the blinders of tradition or failure or past hurts and see in the truest, simplest form what God's original intent for you was, so you can also see God's still-intact intent. God never changes! What He was, He is and will continue to be.

Now let me ask those of you who have and those who want to have children a question. Was your first thought as you were holding them about loving them and hanging out with them, playing on the floor with them, taking them on vacations, and so on, or was it, "I can't wait till they can cut the grass and take out the trash?"

In all of Scripture, God is referred to as King some thirty-something times, but He's referred to as Father more than two hundred and fifty times. Yet most Christians and peoples of the earth in general relate to God with a servant mentality instead of a child's identity as a son or daughter.

It's true we are all created by God, and in that sense, with Him as Creator, we all originate from God, but it's not until after we are born again that we become the very sons and daughters of God. The whole purpose in Jesus taking on the form of a man was to ransom us back by His own blood and restore to us our family fellowship of God.

Father God is not like the Wizard of Oz—all-powerful, all-knowing, and meant to be feared and separate from us. He created us to fellowship with Him. God gave Adam instructions on how to act like Him and then came and walked, talked, and hung out with His family every day in the garden.

Satan's single strategy since his own rebellion caused his fall is to try and separate us from fellowship with Father God, too. Do you really think that the terrible destruction of and attack on the family, marriage, and most particularly the father image in our society is just some big coincidence?

Did you know the very last verse in the Old Testament is a prophecy by Malachi? Basically, it was the last word God spoke to Israel for nearly four hundred years until just before Jesus was born. I want you to see what was on God's heart and what the purpose of Jesus' mission on the earth was all about in a nutshell.

> Behold, I will send you Elijah the prophet before the coming of the great and dreadful day of the Lord. And he will turn The hearts of the fathers to the children, And the hearts of the children to their fathers, Lest I come and strike the earth with a curse. (Malachi 4:5-6)

My loose interpretation of this verse is simply this: Before Jesus' birth and ministry of reconciliation between God and mankind, God set the expectations of what He intended to do. God had John the Baptist prepare the way of the Lord. Jesus, at His baptism in the Jordan, immediately began His ministry with God declaring from heaven, "This is My beloved Son," and from that moment Jesus went out and revealed God as Father and how to make our way back home.

Part of that journey is to restore the family unit on earth, so mankind can see in the natural realm the truths that are represented in the spiritual realm. In the parable of the prodigal son, Jesus tells how the son, while in a far away country, was fooled into believing he was living the good life. After exhausting all of his resources, he begins to reconsider his father's house and thinks of going home. Let's look at it and then consider a few points:

> "About the time his money ran out, a great famine swept over the land, and he began to starve. He persuaded a local farmer to hire him, and the man sent him into his fields to feed the pigs. The young man became so hungry that even the pods he was feeding the pigs looked good to him. But no one gave him anything. When he finally came to his senses, he said to himself, 'At home even the hired servants have food enough to spare, and here I am

dying of hunger! I will go home to my father and say, "Father, I have sinned against both heaven and you, and I am no longer worthy of being called your son. Please take me on as a hired servant."

"So he returned home to his father. And while he was still a long way off, his father saw him coming. Filled with love and compassion, he ran to his son, embraced him, and kissed him. His son said to him, 'Father, I have sinned against both heaven and you, and I am no longer worthy of being called your son.' "But his father said to the servants, 'Quick! Bring the finest robe in the house and put it on him. Get a ring for his finger and sandals for his feet. And kill the calf we have been fattening. We must celebrate with a feast, for this son of mine was dead and has now returned to life. He was lost, but now he is found.' So the party began" (Luke 15:14-24 NLT).

I love what happened here. The son tried to take on the status as a servant when he returned home, but the father was expectantly looking for his son's return, and when they met the father kissed and hugged his lost son. The son began to explain himself and repent, but before he could finish the father interrupted him and with haste began to restore his identity as a son.

Jesus easily explained our separation from fellowship as death and its restoration as being alive again in the last part of this verse. This is the basis for and all that is meant by the term "born again."

According to the heart and attitude of Father God, we are to live our lives as children in fellowship first. That does not mean we don't have things to do. Any responsible parent assigns chores and responsibilities to their children for their growth and development, and so does our Father God. He will discipline us when needed, encourage us when needed, teach us when needed, and provide for us; God is our Father.

I said back in the introduction of this book that Jesus came not only to ransom us and bring us home, but also to reveal the true heart of God to us. When one of the disciples asked Jesus to teach them how to pray, Jesus said, "When you pray, say: Our Father in Heaven..." (Luke 11:2).

Jesus referred to God as His Father and our Father continually throughout the New Testament, which, by the way, seriously irritated the religious leaders of His day. They believed that God was corporately the Father of all Israel, but Jesus came declaring God as a personal Father—first and foremost His Father, and then ours as well, if we would live by faith and accept Jesus as God's Son sent to reconcile us back to God.

There are many references in which Jesus referred to God as our Father. The Lord's Prayer is just one of those references, and another one of my favorites occurs immediately after Jesus' resurrection.

> "Don't cling to me," Jesus said, "for I haven't yet ascended to the Father. But go find my brothers and tell them, '*I am ascending to my Father and your Father, to my God and your God*'" (John 20:17 NLT).

This Scripture and the verses leading up to it have been one of my favorites for nearly forty years because to me it sums up Jesus' whole mission. Jesus had successfully reintroduced and reconciled us back to our Father God.

Worship can take on many forms and have many different purposes; certainly one of those purposes is the simple act of thankfulness. Worship is a wonderful way to honor the Lord and display your love for Him, but fellowship, ah, fellowship is a sweet place of family togetherness.

Faith Declaration: I am a child of God through faith in Christ Jesus. I live my life to exhibit the mannerisms and attitudes of my Father. The more I fellowship with Him, the more I become like Him.

Chapter 19: You Go On and Be Saved, Coleman

For when we were still without strength, in due time Christ died for the ungodly. For scarcely for a righteous man will one die; yet perhaps for a good man someone would even dare to die. But God demonstrates His own love toward us, in that while we were still sinners, Christ died for us. Much more then, having now been justified by His blood, we shall be saved from wrath through Him. For if when we were enemies we were reconciled to God through the death of His Son, much more, having been reconciled, we shall be saved by His life.
—Romans 5:6-10

I'm sure by now you have formed some kind of opinion as to what type of person I must be and how good my life must have been to this point to receive revelation and hear from the Lord like I say I do. You may be considering how wonderful my upbringing must have been and how lovely our family life must have looked, raising four kids and telling them all these wonderful stories while we pastored a church just for kids. I know I have done this myself when I've read other authors or listened to other speakers, and there are some who have had that picture-perfect life. You know, the third-generation preacher who was brought up on the front row, never rebelled, and has been sure of his calling since he was in the sixth grade—but that's not me.

I came from a home broken several times over, went to eleven different schools, lived in more than twenty-five different locations in several different cities and states, and took thirteen different kinds of drugs before I got saved while I was serving in the United States Air Force just a few years after Vietnam.

Consider the Squirrel

I was on a temporary duty assignment at Wright Patterson Air Force Base in Ohio. I had been working with the same five guys for nearly two years; they were like my extended family. It was a Sunday morning and I was watching a preacher on television. Trust me, that was something I had never done before, but there I was in my dorm room still laying in my bunk as I watched.

When he was done preaching, he called people to come up front for prayer, and as I watched people getting up out of their seats, the thought came to me: "Sit up on the end of your bed," to which I thought back, "What the heck for? I've watched the whole thing from right here." But you know, I ended up on the end of my bed, prayed the prayer with everybody else and then confessed, "Thank You, Jesus. I'm now born again."

I couldn't explain what just happened completely; sure, I had been thinking about the direction my life was going and how I wanted to do some things differently, but I hadn't imagined this. I had moved to Georgia with my mom and stepdad during my sophomore year of high school, so growing up in the Bible belt I knew what being "born again" was, or so I thought. But this was different—I actually did it.

Well, I had been crying, so I wanted to go wash my face in the bathroom down the hall, but first I grabbed my pack of cigarettes and opened up my wallet to take out the stash of cocaine that I had in there, and then I headed down the hall.

I walked directly over to one of the stalls and flushed everything down the latrine. Then I walked over to the sink area and from a distance looked in the mirror. It was like I was in slow motion. I just kind of stared at myself for a moment and then walked up real close and grabbed the stainless steel shelf under the mirror and pulled my face to within about three inches of the mirror and looked into my face.

I looked at how bloodshot my eyes were, partly because I had been out partying the night before and partly because I had just been crying pretty hard. I just studied my eyes. I looked at how blue they were, and the slight brown ring that encompassed my pupils. I stared at myself for quite some time, and then I spoke to the man in the mirror: "You don't look any different, Bobby Coleman, but I know you are."

140

Bobby Coleman

I have never forgotten the intensity of that moment. Then I went back to my room and dug out my little New Testament that they gave me when I first joined the service and read all the rest of the day.

The next morning when I walked into the shop, my tech sergeant and all my buddies were there, so I told them what happened. Because I was usually the life of the party, naturally they all thought I was joking and burst out laughing.

"Coleman, you're a crazy man," said one.

"You freaking idiot," said another. Yet out of all the laughter and comments they were making, we could all hear Sergeant "H," as I will call him. He was our boss, and he said, "Hold up ya'll; come here, Coleman."

Tech Sergeant H was from Wheeling, West Virginia, and being from the Bible belt and growing up Southern Baptist, he looked at me and said, "You got born again, bubba?"

"Yes, sir," I replied. And then I went on to tell him I had a dream last night, and that all of them were in it too.

He just looked at me smugly and said, "Tell me about your dream, Coleman."

I told him: "I was running down a city street and y'all were chasing me and were yelling at me, and as I was running the street kept getting narrower, and finally it looked like y'all had me cornered. We were all in an alley and there was a wall in front of me and you were all running toward me. I jumped up and grabbed the top of the wall, and as I did I started to pull myself over, and then y'all grabbed my legs. As we struggled and pulled against each other, I woke up."

They were all just looking at me with wide eyes and a dumbfounded look on their faces. I stood there, looking back at them, shrugging my shoulders and said, "I don't even know what it means, but it sure was weird."

Nobody was laughing now, and that's when Sergeant H said, "I know exactly what it means. You go on and be saved. We ain't gonna hold you back. In your dream you wanted to escape and do something

141

new, and we didn't like it and were trying to make you stay with us. That's why we grabbed your legs, but we ain't gonna hold you back. You go on and be saved, Coleman!"

Like I said, we had been together as a unit for nearly two years and had not been separated for other assignments, not even once. Yet the very next day Tuesday, March 20, 1984, Sergeant H showed up while I was working in a manhole system and said, "Hey kid, get up here, you're going back to the Griff!" That was Griffiss Air Force Base, our home duty station, and the next morning I was gone, just like in my dream.

The very next Sunday back in Rome, New York, I went to church for the first time in many years. I met my wife, Lisa, there, and we were married the following year in July, 1985. We started Bible college in the fall of that same year.

You know, I've shared my testimony hundreds of times, but until I wrote it down for this book, I never considered just how prophetic Tech Sergeant H's interpretation of my dream and the events at the shop that morning really were. After all, that was the first time I had confessed before men my newfound faith in Jesus Christ.

Now back to the mirror. Twice over the last forty years—and neither time as a premeditated event—I have found myself with my face back in the mirror with that same intensity. Both were during critical struggles in my life—one concerning my faith itself and the other during a very difficult time in my own marriage.

I had to speak to myself and recall what I believed: Jesus Christ came into my life that Sunday morning, March 18, and saved me from myself. He delivered me from a life I didn't want, and I needed the memory of the tears and intensity of that first original moment to hold my ground when I had come to the end of my rope in these other two situations.

King David had a time when he, too, had come to the end of himself, and although he did not have a mirror to look into, he definitely looked into his own soul and had to speak to himself.

Now it happened, when David and his men came to Ziklag, on the third day, that the Amalekites had invaded the South and Ziklag, attacked Ziklag and burned it with fire, and had taken captive the women and those who were there, from small to great; they did not kill anyone, but carried them away and went their way. So David and his men came to the city, and there it was, burned with fire; and their wives, their sons, and their daughters had been taken captive. Then David and the people who were with him lifted up their voices and wept, until they had no more power to weep. And David's two wives, Ahinoam the Jezreelitess, and Abigail the widow of Nabal the Carmelite, had been taken captive. Now David was greatly distressed, for the people spoke of stoning him, because the soul of all the people was grieved, every man for his sons and his daughters. But David strengthened himself in the Lord his God.

Then David said to Abiathar the priest, Ahimelech's son, "Please bring the ephod here to me." And Abiathar brought the ephod to David. So David inquired of the Lord, saying, "Shall I pursue this troop? Shall I overtake them?"

And He answered him, "Pursue, for you shall surely overtake *them* and without fail recover *all* (1 Samuel 30:1-8).

Then David attacked them from twilight until the evening of the next day. Not a man of them escaped, except four hundred young men who rode on camels and fled. So David recovered all that the Amalekites had carried away, and David rescued his two wives. And nothing of theirs was lacking, either small or great, sons or daughters, spoil or anything which they had taken from them; *David recovered all.* (1 Samuel 30:17-19).

In my own life, as you well know by now, I have done what it is recorded here that David did. I have encouraged myself; I have spoken to myself and repeated who God says I am and even who people I trust say that I am. Then I have had to act like the champion I profess to be, and like David I have pursued, overtaken, and recovered all.

Making a decision to live your life for Christ isn't a get-out-of-jail-free card by which we escape the difficulties of life, it is normal in life to have challenges, but it's not normal to suffer defeat. As I have said at different points throughout this book, we are eternal spirit who have a soul and live in a body. Our spirit is going to live on long after we surrender our bodies back to the earth. Accepting the finished work of the cross of Jesus Christ is all about you being reconciled back to the Father and having your fellowship with Him restored.

It bears repeating here that eternal life isn't just about the length of your life, it's also about the quality of your life here and now, and He who is the Author of all life certainly knows how to make it worth living. I want to close this book with this last passage of Scripture which best describes what took place in my life starting on March 18, 1984, and continuing to this day by you reading this book.

> Therefore, if anyone is in Christ, he is a new creation; old things have passed away; behold, all things have become new. Now all things are of God, who has reconciled us to Himself through Jesus Christ, and has given us the ministry of reconciliation, that is, that God was in Christ reconciling the world to Himself, not imputing their trespasses to them, and has committed to us the word of reconciliation. Now then, we are ambassadors for Christ, as though God were pleading through us: we implore you on Christ's behalf, be reconciled to God. For He made Him who knew no sin to be sin for us, that we might become the righteousness of God in Him (2 Corinthians 5:17-21).

And so it is that I find myself about the Father's business, using His words through the pages of this book to reconcile the world back to Himself. If that's a place that you want to be as well, then join me in a simple prayer of salvation. Then just as I have for more than forty years now, you too can enjoy a new life in Christ!

If you are already a Christian, I pray your walk and life have been strengthened and your purpose and passions renewed. Live your life on purpose, follow the leadings of the Holy Spirit with confidence, and go—go be about our Father's business.

Faith Declaration: I have been crucified with Christ; it is no longer I who live, but Christ lives in me, and the life which I now live in the flesh I live by faith in the Son of God, who loved me and gave Himself for me.

Section IV Review Page: Believing

Writing this book has been an eighteen-month process (if you consider the editing, it's probably longer) that has challenged me in each of the four focuses we have experienced together. My own desire to move forward was birthed out of struggle, and once I determined that I didn't want to get stuck and going back would serve me no purpose, forward was my only option.

How you discovered my book, I believe, was God's great love for you, challenging you in much the same way. Sure, it may have seemed that the stories I have shared made our lives exciting, and certainly it was at times, but much of life is mundane. It's taking out the trash and doing the dishes; it's going to work every day and paying the bills; and occasionally, yet deliberately, it's experiencing the excitement of life. The moral from Chapter 13 is ever so true. Man measures time by seconds and minutes; God measures by seasons and moments, which is why we must always choose to move forward, enjoy each day, and continue to grow!

I pray that the sections on seeing and hearing how God works in our lives have moved you to a deeper desire to believe. We've covered an awful lot together, and I pray that you are free, more encouraged, and more determined than ever to live out the words of the apostle Paul as he neared his ending point: "I have fought the good fight, I have finished the race, and I have remained faithful. And now the prize awaits me—the crown of righteousness, which the Lord, the righteous Judge, will give me on the day of his return. And the prize is not just for me but for all who eagerly look forward to his appearing." (2 Timothy 4:7-8 NLT).

So use the principles you have discovered while reading *Consider the Squirrel* to encourage your own loved ones, friends, and neighbors.

Consider the Squirrel

Or, just as we gave away the two-sided maps at the music festival, get your own little supply of this book and give them away so others can experience what you have.

Chapter 20: A Collection of Prayers

If you openly declare that Jesus is Lord and believe in your heart
that God raised him from the dead, you will be saved. For it is by
believing in your heart that you are made right with God, and it is
by openly declaring your faith that you are saved.
—Romans 10:9-10 NLT

A Prayer for Salvation

Dear God,

I come to You in the name of Jesus. I believe in my heart that Jesus died on the cross for me—to break the power of sin and death over my life. I ask You to forgive me of my sins and to cleanse me from all unrighteousness. I confess with my mouth that Jesus is Lord and Savior of my life. Thank You for saving me. I accept this initial work of the Holy Spirit in my life and now believe that I am a child of God and You are my heavenly Father. In Jesus' name I pray. Amen.

A Prayer of Rededication

Dear heavenly Father,

I know in my heart that Jesus is Lord and that I have been saved. According to Your Word I was sealed by the Holy Spirit on the day of my salvation and that is an unchangeable fact, but I have sinned and ask You to forgive me. I want to restore my fellowship with You. I can't change what I have done or even how or why I allowed myself to be pulled away and live the way I have been living. I'm counting on 1 John 1:9, which says You would forgive me if I confessed my sin to You, that You would cleanse me from all unrighteousness. I know the blood of Jesus was shed just for this purpose and by faith I receive Your forgiveness. Thank You, Father; I will not allow my past to keep me from moving forward, for he who the Son sets free is free indeed. I am free! In Jesus' name. Amen.

A Prayer of Consecration

Father God,

Galatians 2:20 says that I have been crucified with Christ; it is no longer I who live, but Christ who lives in me; and the *life* which I now live in the flesh I live by faith in the Son of God, who loved me and gave Himself for me. Father, in the garden Jesus knew the task that was ahead of Him. He knew why He came to the earth, but He still struggled with the intensity of the pain and suffering He knew He was about to endure. And yet He looked beyond that to the joy it was going to bring—our ability to be reconciled to You. Father, reveal Your purposes and plans for my life to me, so I can walk them out and bring glory to Your name. Help me overcome and conquer the things I struggle with, just as Jesus did, so I too can proclaim, "Not my will, Father, but Yours be done in my life!" In Jesus' name! Amen.

About the Author

Bobby and Lisa Coleman pastor the River Gainesville Church in Florida and co-founded Open Skies Ministries, which they operate from their ministry base, The Open Skies Ranch. The ranch exists to refresh and train believers for revival, hosting ministers and their families, conferences for men, women, and married couples, youth and children's summer camps, and specialized ministry for veterans and first responders. Their ministry has one main purpose: to see all come to the saving knowledge of God and to be baptized in the Holy Spirit and fire, and to make disciples, equipping them to spread the gospel worldwide.

Ministry Information

For ministry information or to schedule revival meetings with Bobby and Lisa please email a request to our official ministry email: openskiesranchflorida@gmail.com.